CREATING HIGH VALUE PMOS

YOUR ESSENTIAL GUIDE

Brendon Baker

First Published 2021
Paperback ISBN: 978-0-6451227-4-9
eBook ISBN: 978-0-6451227-3-2

CONTENTS

Your PMO GamePlan

Appendix

CREATING HIGH VALUE PMOS
YOUR ESSENTIAL GUIDE

1

So, You Want to Create a High Value PMO?

Congratulations.

Almost every organisation these days has tried to build a functioning Project, Program or Portfolio Management Office at least once ...And almost every organisation has failed. It seems as though most PMOs are cursed from the start.

Bucking the trend requires something radically different. ...And someone bold to drive it.

If you think that could be you, then read on.

You are about to embark on quite a journey.

You will laugh. You may cry.

But most importantly if you do it right, you will be genuinely helping people. (And, as an added bonus, you will truly prove that you are someone *'who can make magic happen')*.

So, reader, what landed you here?

- Perhaps you are frustrated with the lack of logic in allocating change investment?
- Or maybe you are staring at an overwhelming number of reports, systems, frameworks and methodologies?
- Do your project managers need a capability boost?
- Or is it that the information you need just isn't there?
- Maybe you are about to commence a large program of work?
- Or is it just chaos – and your projects are running amok.

No matter the reason you are here, I've got some great news. This guide will help.

This guide is for you if you have been tasked with setting up a new PMO, and you want to do it right.

Equally, this guide is for you if your office is well established but you just aren't getting the results you expected or need.

In short - this guide is for you if you need to create entirely new levels of value through your PMO.

PLEASE NOTE: This guide does NOT replace the current swarth of textbooks that explain what a PMO is, what a project is, or any of the many different things that they do. So, if this is your first foray into the world of PMOs, I suggest you read this book, then read one of those ones, then come back and read this book again. With that combined knowledge you will have the full picture. **Those books will tell you what you need to build, and this book shows you how to make it successful.**

But why should you listen to me?

...Simple. I have made the mistakes, delved into why others failed, and using those learnings I have driven consistent success across over $10 Billion in transformational projects and programs across a range of industries. This has included public infrastructure, business/cultural transformations, whole of government initiatives, shared service implementations, restructures, privatisations and sales, process overhauls, technology deployments, social policy and more.

More importantly for you, I have built and coached Project, Program and Portfolio Offices of all sizes. From organisation-wide behemoths through to offices that consist of just one person. From big to small, I've helped them create new value.

I have learned what works (and what doesn't), and here in this guide, I decode those years of experience into what you must know to create a truly High Value PMO. But before we do, let's look at why most PMOs fail. For those of you that have been around PMOs a while – this may feel all too familiar.

Some Quick Housekeeping

- Wherever I refer to a 'PMO', you are welcome to read that as Portfolio Management Office, Program Management Office, Project Management Office, or any related derivative. The principles and steps in this guide work no matter the level of PMO you are operating at.
- Throughout this guide I'll be using the terms 'Project', 'Program' and 'Initiative' interchangeably to represent a concerted effort to change something, whether internal or external to your organisation.
- This guide is delivery method agnostic, i.e., it works no matter which methodology you are supporting (agile, waterfall, hybrid, etc.)
- The guide applies and works for PMOs of all sizes. From one to one hundred people, you're never too small or too big to add value to your organisation.

1

THE PMO CURSE

2

Know Your Enemy – The Administrative Death Cycle

"Action must be taken,
We don't need the key, we'll break in,
Something must be done,"
Know Your Enemy, Rage Against the Machine

Introducing the Administrative Death Cycle

Grim name, I know.

But the more you work in the PMO space, the more you get used to seeing organisational graveyards filled with the failed PMOs that came before you. Unless you are operating in a new program of work, I can almost guarantee someone else (or maybe even you) has tried to set up a PMO in your exact space.

In fact, across my experience, most organisations I've helped have had an average of 3-5 previous attempts at getting a PMO right! Given that each of these attempts average a 2-3 year lifespan, that's a LOT of wasted time and money.

It wasn't long after noticing these graveyards, that I decided to start delving in and conducting PMO post-mortems. Like an archeologist delving through the remains of my client's ancient cities, I unearthed the PMO skeletons, avoided the zombies, aired out the tombs, outrun the boulders and ultimately...

... I discovered the pattern.

I'd like to share it with you.

So, let's walk through it. Step by step, and you can tell me if any of this sounds familiar.

First, There is No Clear, Informed Picture of Project Progress

This is our first state. Projects exist but are generally free to operate independently and in their own way.

Common characteristics that are often found in this state, include:

- A lack of project investment logic
- A lack of project confidence
- A lack of consistent process, and
- Low project management maturity

Usually there is a mix of the above. An organisation may exist like this for a while, but over time the frustrations that stem from chaos build up until someone with enough clout (and a budget) says:

"No one knows what is going on! We need a PMO."

Which leads us to our next state.

A PMO is Stood Up

Its initial focus can vary but it normally starts with an effort to build consistent processes and some sort of reporting. Typically it has a mission along the lines of:

"We will drive consistency and visibility"

So, the PMO takes the next logical step.

PMO Produces Metrics and Reports

To achieve its mission, the PMO starts producing reports and metrics to monitor the projects under its remit. What it finds is often a mixed bag. Some projects are healthy. Others aren't.

The issue is that after a few months of consistent processes and pretty reports, the unhealthy projects don't seem to be improving.

So, the PMO thinks:

"The projects aren't improving... We need more assurance."

The PMO Increases Rigour - More Metrics, More Tests, Greater Hurdles

The PMO, eager to please its stressed executives, dials up its health check and assurance programs.

More checks, more gates, more oversight.

Which of course creates

...More delays,

...Slower Processes,

...And ultimately overburdens both the PMO and the Projects.

Suddenly, the PMO has found itself 'policing' projects. It has created a 'command and control' culture. Smothered with bureaucracy, the projects naturally think:

"This is overly cumbersome."

Which eventually leads to discontent.

Project Managers Subvert the PMO Systems and Complain in Corridors to Project Executives

Gradually it begins. The shadow processes. The work arounds.

Projects subvert the now cumbersome processes. Despite the PMOs persistent, but now, often cynical attempts at driving adherence – projects are now resorting to seeking forgiveness rather than permission just so things still get done!

Slowly but surely the PMO is neutered. Then one day someone with a notable amount of office clout mentions that:

> *"We would be faster without the PMO.*
> *The PMO is a hindrance – and an expensive one at that!"*

And just like that, the fate of the PMO is sealed. It's death-bound.

PMO Disbanded

The PMO is closed down. Contractors are let go and employees are redeployed.

Another PMO is buried in the organisational graveyard. The grave is unmarked. A stone is not risen. No songs are sung.

...A couple of years then pass, and a new executive comes in. They look around and notice the lack of a clear, informed picture of projects.

They think:

> *"No one knows what is going on! We need a PMO."*

And off we go again!

Visualising the Cycle

The figure on the next page demonstrates the clear progression through each of these states.

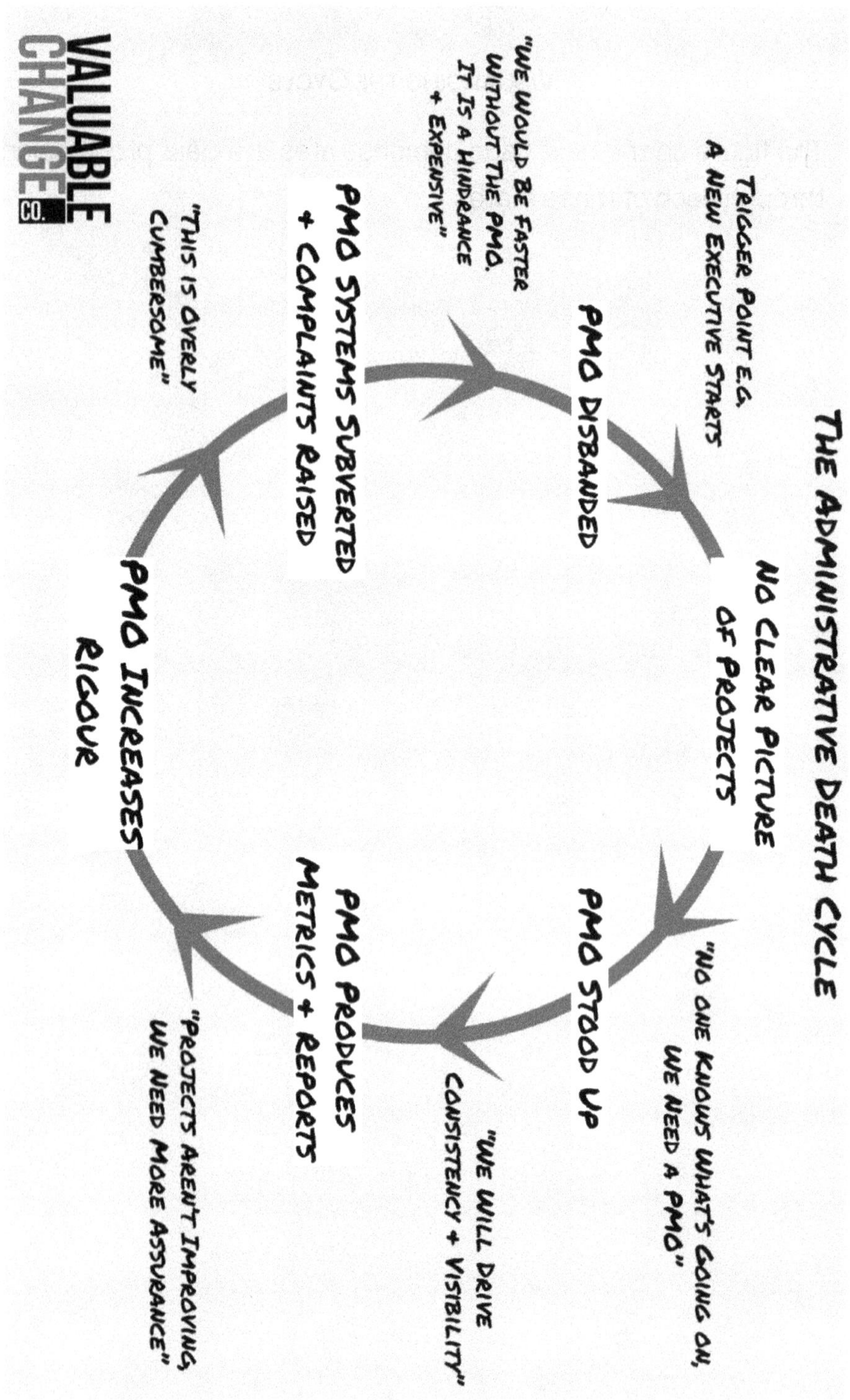

THE ADMINISTRATIVE DEATH CYCLE
NO CLEAR PICTURE OF PROJECTS
"NO ONE KNOWS WHAT'S GOING ON, WE NEED A PMO"
PMO STOOD UP
"WE WILL DRIVE CONSISTENCY + VISIBILITY"
PMO PRODUCES METRICS + REPORTS
"PROJECTS AREN'T IMPROVING, WE NEED MORE ASSURANCE"
PMO INCREASES RIGOUR
"THIS IS OVERLY CUMBERSOME"
PMO SYSTEMS SUBVERTED + COMPLAINTS RAISED
"WE WOULD BE FASTER WITHOUT THE PMO. IT IS A HINDRANCE + EXPENSIVE"
PMO DISBANDED
TRIGGER POINT E.G. A NEW EXECUTIVE STARTS
VALUABLE CHANGE CO.

So, How Do We Break the Cycle?

Simple. We need to change the fatal assumption that greater assurance = greater projects.

It just doesn't.

So, how do we break the cycle? We must create a break point.

The best place for it is soon after we stand up our PMO, but realistically, we can create this breakpoint any time before the PMO is disbanded. (Though, the earlier the better).

The key thing we must adjust is our thinking. We must avoid falling into the trap of

> *"The projects aren't improving... We need more assurance."*

And instead, we need to pivot to

> *"The projects aren't improving... What new value can we offer to increase their capability?"*

It is only through this new way of thinking that we can enter a new cycle. One without PMO death.

We will enter 'The High Value Service Cycle'.

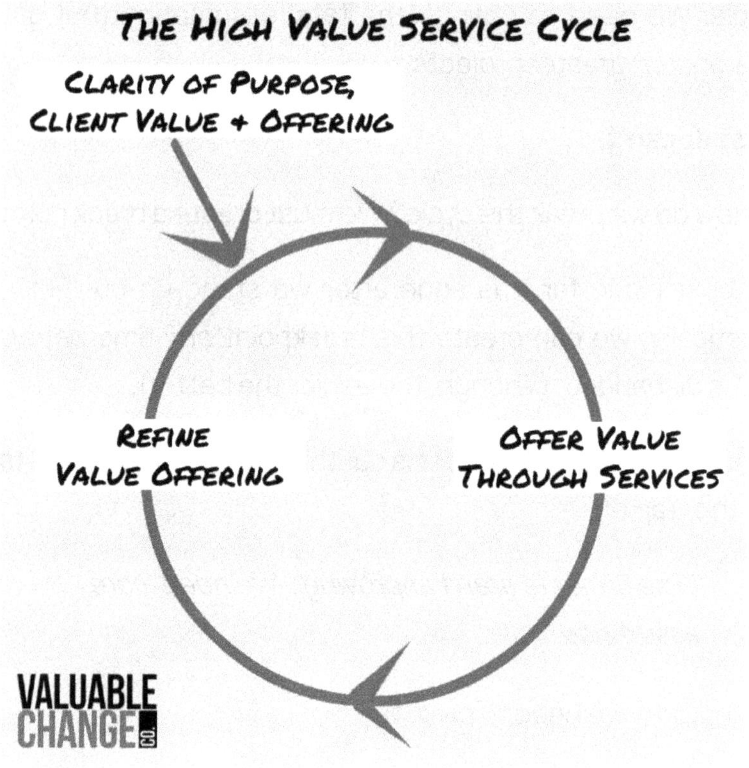

It is only through the High Value Service Cycle that we will create PMOs that last.

To bring all this together for those visual learners amongst us, the figure below shows what happens when we break out of the administrative death cycle.

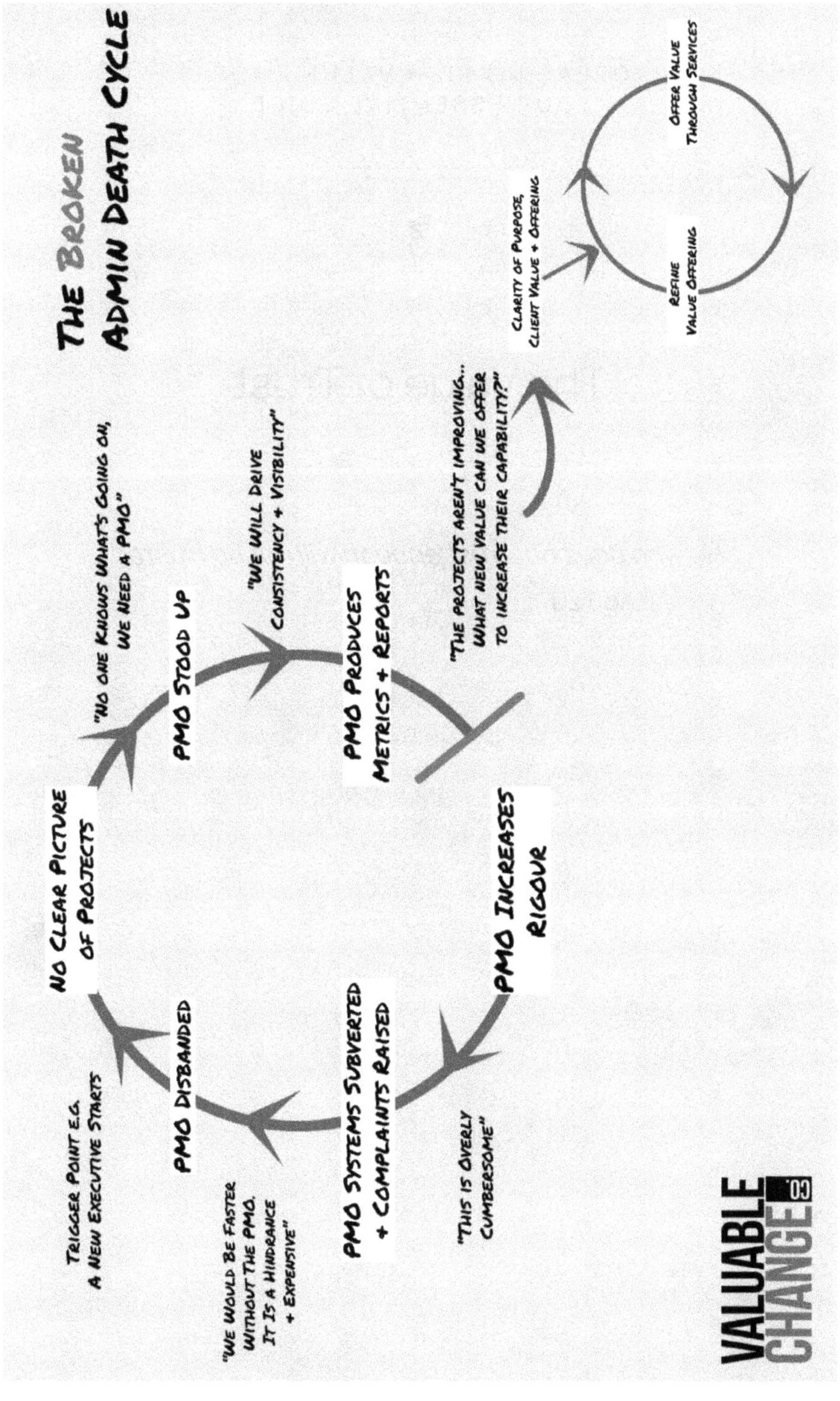
THE BROKEN
ADMIN DEATH CYCLE
NO CLEAR PICTURE OF PROJECTS
"NO ONE KNOWS WHAT'S GOING ON, WE NEED A PMO"
PMO STOOD UP
"WE WILL DRIVE CONSISTENCY + VISIBILITY"
PMO PRODUCES METRICS + REPORTS
"THE PROJECTS AREN'T IMPROVING... WHAT NEW VALUE CAN WE OFFER TO INCREASE THEIR CAPABILITY?"
CLARITY OF PURPOSE, CLIENT VALUE + OFFERING
OFFER VALUE THROUGH SERVICES
REFINE VALUE OFFERING
PMO INCREASES RIGOUR
"THIS IS OVERLY CUMBERSOME"
PMO SYSTEMS SUBVERTED + COMPLAINTS RAISED
"WE WOULD BE FASTER WITHOUT THE PMO. IT IS A HINDRANCE + EXPENSIVE"
PMO DISBANDED
TRIGGER POINT E.G. A NEW EXECUTIVE STARTS
VALUABLE CHANGE CO.

3

The Value of Trust

"He who does not trust enough will not be trusted,"
Lao Tzu

The Value Continuum

Another way to think about this is on a plot of value and trust.

When there is a lack of a PMO or similar body, this creates our first zone: Chaos. This is a low trust, low value environment.

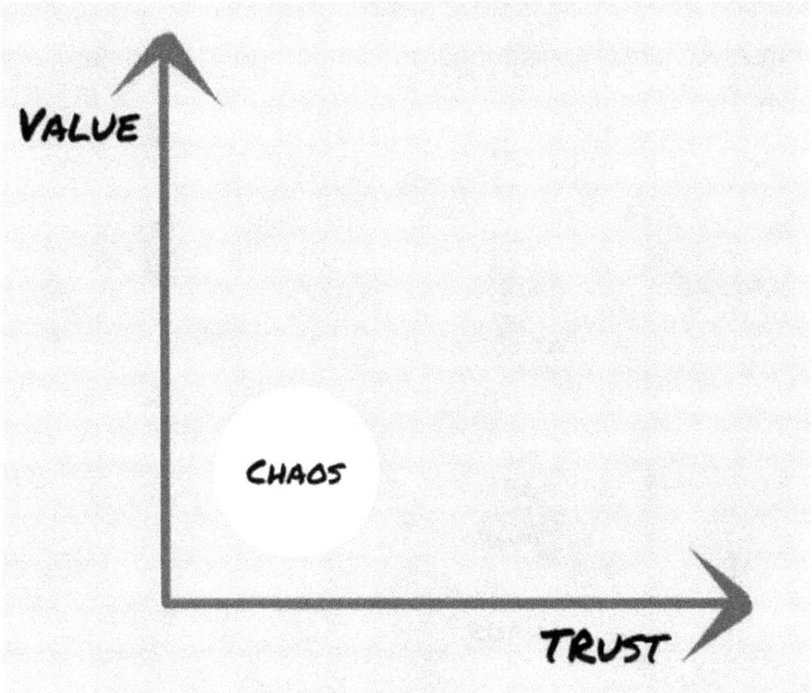

As we explored in the previous chapter, many PMOs manage to shift the environment into a medium trust, medium value environment. They do this using a 'command & control' focus – i.e. "You must do…"

As we have already seen, PMOs with a command and control, assurance-based focus have a short shelf-life. They quickly find themselves an organisational nuisance and are ultimately put down.

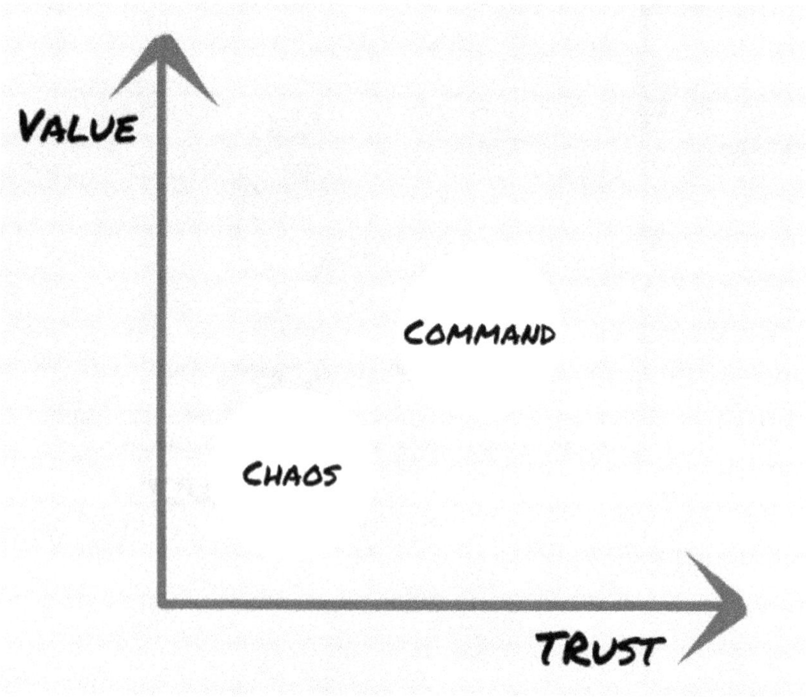

Our aim in setting up or maturing our PMO is to reach High Value, High Trust. We do this by centering value and service into our PMO's very core.

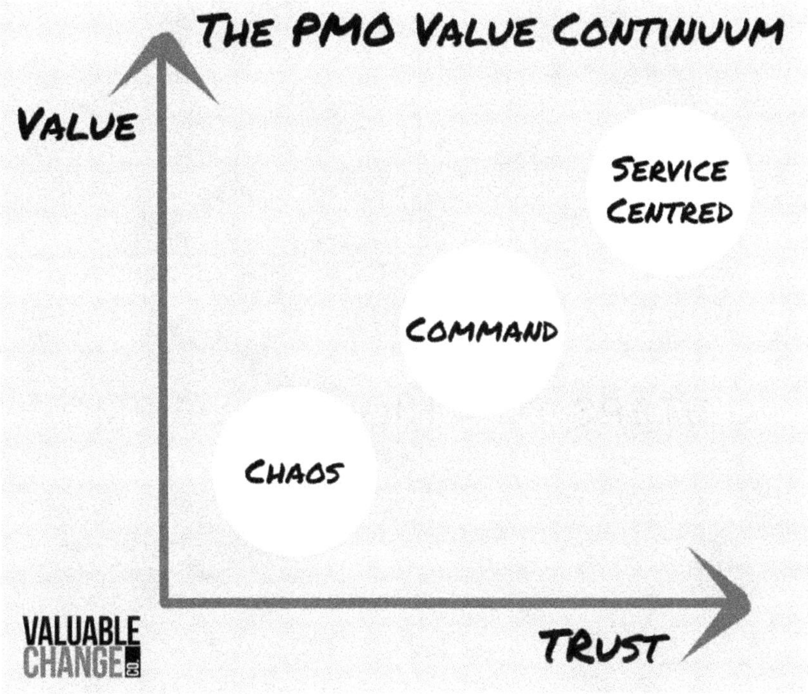

So how do we do it?

This is what the rest of this guide will give you.

3 STEPS TO A HIGH VALUE PMO

4

The 3 Steps

"Don't Panic."

The Hitchhikers Guide to the Galaxy,

Douglas Adams

A Quick Overview.

Over the remainder of this guide, I will walk you through the 3 steps that will ensure you aim straight at that High Trust, High Value, Service Focused Target.

I don't want you driving blind, so over the page you will find a summary of the 3 steps that will underpin your PMO success.

The 3 Steps To A High Value PMO
Get Clear
- Your Purpose
- Your Clients
- Your Offering
Rally The People
- Build Team Momentum
- Enlist Internal Influencers
- Foster External Community
Avoid Cultural Traps
- Stagnation
- Dysfunctional Monopolies
- 'Us' + 'Them'
- The 7 Deadly Fears

5

Step 1: Get Clear

"To know thyself is the beginning of wisdom."
Socrates

Before we can do anything else, we must first get absurdly clear on the core elements of our PMO. There are three elements to this.

1. Clarity of Purpose
2. Clarity of Client
3. Clarity of Offering

Warning: Do not skip this step.

If you have ever done yoga or weightlifting, you will know that both are exponentially harder with a weak abdominal core. This is similarly true for creating a High Value PMO. It is exponentially more difficult to rally your people, create learning and growth and fend off cultural traps without a strong core. People often underestimate how easy the remainder of the work becomes once the clarity work is complete.

Clarity of Purpose

Why does your PMO exist? (And if it doesn't yet – why should it?!)

What is its purpose?

Your purpose needs to be so clear that every member of your PMO (and ideally your client base) should be able to answer this instinctively.

The Power of Purpose

Let's take a little detour to touch on what a good, clear purpose can help you achieve.

In 2008 a group of friends hanging out in their living room came across 2 numbers that truly shocked them.

- 900 Million people across the world didn't have access to clean drinking water.
- Globally, countries with plenty of safe drinking water spent over $50 Billion a year on bottled water.

Initially this group of friends found this polarity ridiculous - until they had a bold idea –

> *'What if we could connect these two numbers?!'*

> *'What if we could start a business selling bottled water where 100% of the profits went to connecting these 900 Million people with clean drinking water?'.*

And so, 'Thankyou.' was born. Despite only having $1000 to their names, this group of friends quickly secured a bottler, packager and distributor. Within 5 years, through sheer public driven momentum, they had grown to 14 products and were stocked in most of Australia's largest retailers and supermarkets.

Within 10 years they had launched a best selling book based on their own start up story, and had used the book to make an international expansion.

'Thankyou.' are clear on their purpose.

> *"End poverty in this lifetime".*

Without clarity of purpose, these friends would still be sitting in that living room - appalled at the numbers on the TV in front of them.

Finding Your Purpose

How do we get to the heart of your PMO purpose?

By answering 2 simple questions.

1. Why do you exist? (i.e., what was the catalyst for the PMO's creation?), and
2. What makes you special? (i.e., what makes your unit different from the rest of the organisation?)

Let's delve into these.

Why Do You Exist?

Be real here.

Why does your PMO exist? (Or Why is it about to?)

Is it as simple as *"the projects are a mess, and the organisation needs some help?"* If so, we can put a positive spin on that and arrive with a purpose along the lines of:

> *"We create clarity across the project portfolio."*

Or perhaps your purpose is to inform key decision makers. If so, then perhaps your PMO purpose is closer to:

> *"We drive great decisions by ensuring the right information is there at the right time."*

Or maybe your PMO is multi-focused, but it has a strong capability improvement slant. That might look like this:

> *"We promote great project management through ongoing support and growing organisational change capability."*

Your catalyst needs to be reflected in your purpose. You need to deeply and clearly understand exactly what problem your PMO is trying to solve.

WHAT MAKES YOU SPECIAL?

No, I don't mean that in a 'we are all unique snowflakes' type of way.

Rather, what we are looking for is: what exactly is in your PMO's remit that isn't in anyone else's? What is your unique obligation within the organisation?

What may initially seem self-evident often isn't once you dig into it.

Let's look at a quick example.

Say your PMO is tasked with overseeing a portfolio of change projects. What exactly is uniquely yours?

Project reporting? - Maybe not. After all, projects are usually reported on by Finance and sometimes even as part of Strategic and Annual reporting processes.

Training and uplift? – Again, maybe not. Learning and Development may well be offering something already.

What about project investment and governance? – Again, possibly not. There may be existing gateway, approval and/or finance allocation processes in place.

To be clear - the intent here isn't to get into the weeds and have you specifying something like the below:

"*So we do project management training... but, not the training that L&D offers, just the training they don't offer. At the moment that's training on project gates and how to log an issue and a risk*".

But rather, the question – 'what makes you special' is about helping you dial into your purpose.

What will your PMO do **better** than anyone else in your organisation?

Use that as your starting point.

How To Use Your Purpose

Now, while it may seem self-evident, we don't often think about how we can best leverage our purpose. It's either put on a wall and forgotten... or worse, put in a drawer and forgotten. I implore you, don't just file this away. It's a crucial tool for your use.

First, your purpose shapes what success looks like for your PMO. It quick-starts your target and goal setting efforts and underpins any strategic planning work you undertake.

Second, and perhaps even more powerfully, it enables you to say 'No' to anything not aligned to your purpose. It is difficult to overstate how crucial the ability to say 'No' is in the PMO world. The scope of what a PMO can do is so large, and resources are almost always limited.

An absurdly clear purpose helps you set expectations on what you will be excellent at, while ringfencing your scope to avoid the cacophony of distractions on the way.

A Common Trap: A Broad, Meaningless Purpose

A broad purpose usually shows a willingness to do everything for everyone. **Avoid this. It will be your undoing**.

Successful PMOs know the power of focus. This will make or break your success.

Do a few things well instead of all things poorly. Chances are that you simply aren't staffed up enough to do it all.

Clarity of Client

Now it's time to move to your clients. To this you may say:

> *"But Brendon, we are just an internal unit? We don't have any clients..."*

And to that I would reply *"Nonsense!"*

A High Value PMO is one that knows who it serves, and even more importantly, what their clients need.

Let's do a quick thought experiment. First, come up with a list of the top 3 key stakeholder groups for your PMO. Common answers here are usually along the lines of 'Executives', 'Project Managers' and 'Procurement' – but don't feel you need to copy these. The top 3 must be right for your organisation and context.

Next, take a moment and pivot your thinking. Try to imagine you and your PMO as a vendor, and that those three stakeholder groups are your 3 most valuable customers. Feel free to anthropomorphise these groups and turn them into customer archetypes. E.g., perhaps you have an Edwina the Executive, Peter the Project Manager and Petunia from Procurement.

Select one of your archetypes. Mentally flesh out their back story. Do your best to put yourself in their shoes. Imagine their typical day, their stressors, their successes. Then ask yourself:

"What problem(s) can your PMO solve for them?"

Don't come up with a laundry list here – just consider the top 1-3 priorities that will have the most immediate impact.

Then, grab a sheet of paper and create 4 columns. In the first column, title it *"Who Are We Serving?"* and enter your archetype's name. In the second, title it, *"What Problem Are We Solving?"* and list down those top 1-3 problems that your PMO can help them with.

I've put together an example for you below.

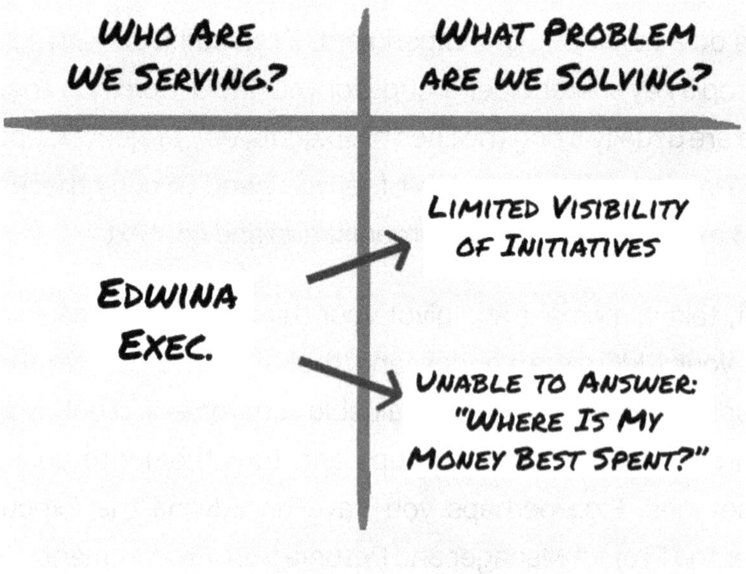

WHO ARE WE SERVING?
WHAT PROBLEM ARE WE SOLVING?
EDWINA EXEC.
LIMITED VISIBILITY OF INITIATIVES
UNABLE TO ANSWER: "WHERE IS MY MONEY BEST SPENT?"

Now we can take it a step further. We are going to visualise what success for this archetypical client looks like. What does it mean when each of the problems we listed are solved? Have a go at describing this new reality and put it in column 3, which we will title

'What Does Success Look Like?'. Feel free to link it up with the previous problems. I've done similar in the example below.

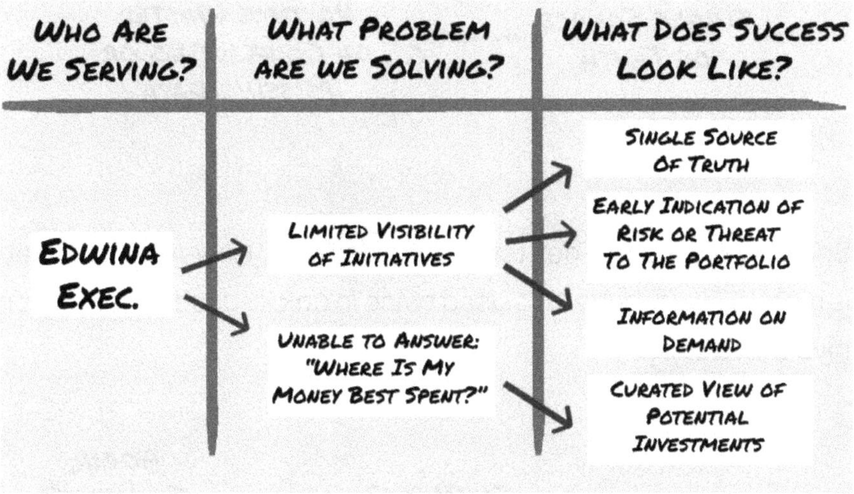
WHO ARE WE SERVING?
WHAT PROBLEM ARE WE SOLVING?
WHAT DOES SUCCESS LOOK LIKE?
EDWINA EXEC.
LIMITED VISIBILITY OF INITIATIVES
UNABLE TO ANSWER: "WHERE IS MY MONEY BEST SPENT?"
SINGLE SOURCE OF TRUTH
EARLY INDICATION OF RISK OR THREAT TO THE PORTFOLIO
INFORMATION ON DEMAND
CURATED VIEW OF POTENTIAL INVESTMENTS

Finally, the fourth column, which we will title '*How Does This Help Them?*', is the value this new reality will bring for this client archetype. Now there's a little trick you can use here.

This is the spot where most of us get stuck at the superficial. So, I've got a little technique to help you ensure you are identifying the true value to your client. It's just 2 simple words:

'So What?!'

Using 'So What' we are able to drill down to the real core value offering. All you have to do is take one of those new realities you have listed and ask yourself 'So What?'. To see what I mean, let's do one together.

SINGLE SOURCE OF TRUTH
SO WHAT?
NO TIME WASTED ON CONFLICTING OR MISSING DATA

See how we start to get towards value here? However, 'So What' is most powerful when it's used twice in quick succession, so let's give that a shot.

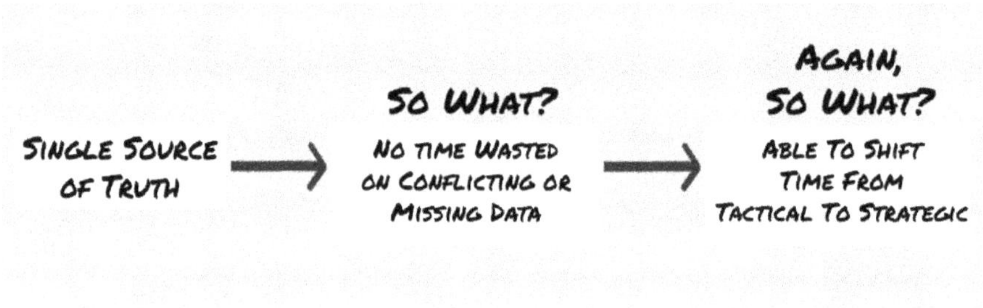
SINGLE SOURCE OF TRUTH
SO WHAT?
NO TIME WASTED ON CONFLICTING OR MISSING DATA
AGAIN, SO WHAT?
ABLE TO SHIFT TIME FROM TACTICAL TO STRATEGIC

Pretty cool right?

Let's do another one together.

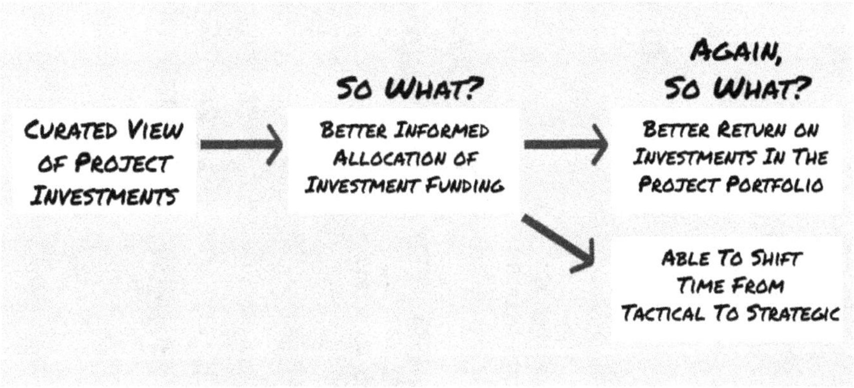

Here we have two points of notable value – however you may have noticed something between this example and the last. Although we started at two different new realities - we arrived at the same value. *"Able to shift time from tactical to strategic".* This is exactly why we map this out for our clients. It shows us what the ultimate value we are providing is – and the various ways we can help them get there.

To finish off this example, after some slight rearranging, we end up with something like the figure on the next page.

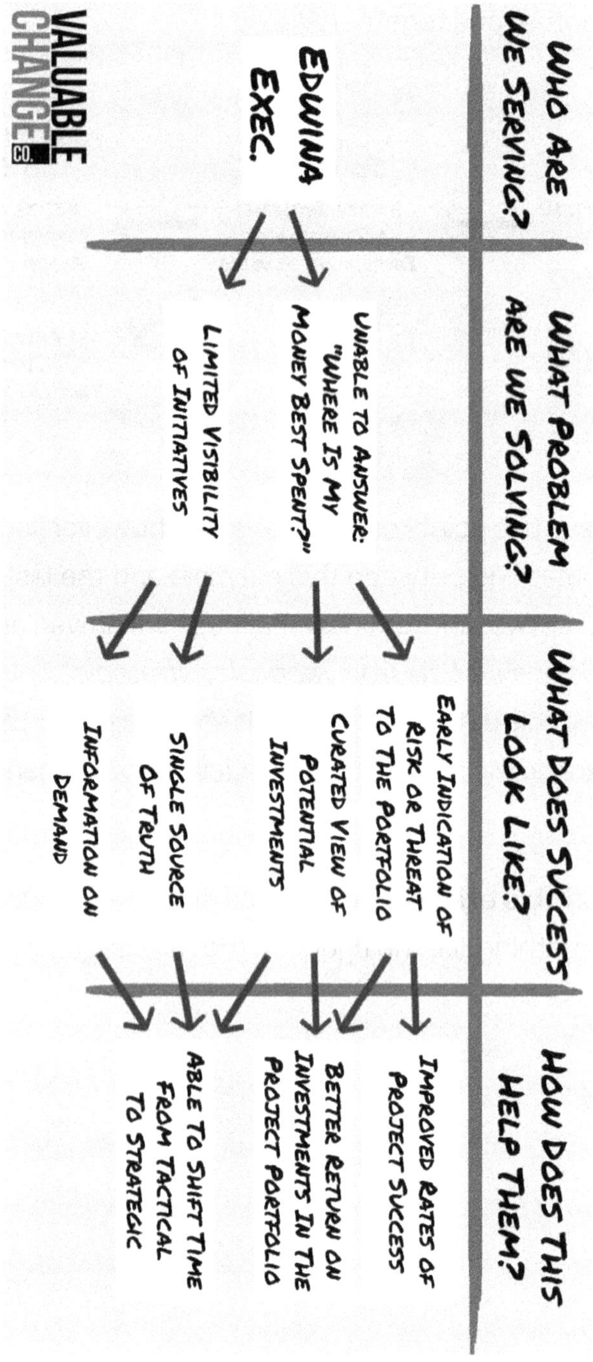
WHO ARE WE SERVING?
EDWINA EXEC.
WHAT PROBLEM ARE WE SOLVING?
UNABLE TO ANSWER: "WHERE IS MY MONEY BEST SPENT?"
LIMITED VISIBILITY OF INITIATIVES
WHAT DOES SUCCESS LOOK LIKE?
EARLY INDICATION OF RISK OR THREAT TO THE PORTFOLIO
CURATED VIEW OF POTENTIAL INVESTMENTS
SINGLE SOURCE OF TRUTH
INFORMATION ON DEMAND
HOW DOES THIS HELP THEM?
IMPROVED RATES OF PROJECT SUCCESS
BETTER RETURN ON INVESTMENTS IN THE PROJECT PORTFOLIO
ABLE TO SHIFT TIME FROM TACTICAL TO STRATEGIC
VALUABLE CHANGE CO.

We can then repeat this process for the other 2 key client archetypes we are serving.

A few notes when creating client clarity:

- Try not to produce these value maps in isolation. It is almost always worthwhile to include actual representatives from your client groups in these value clarity exercises.
- If, throughout this process you find that your purpose no longer makes as much sense as it originally did when you drafted it - then feel free to revisit it. Working through these three clarity steps is often iterative.

Now that we know what success looks like for our client, we can move to how we are going to help them achieve it – our service offerings.

Clarity of Offering

Would you do business with you?

By this I mean, if you pivot your thinking, and rather than considering the processes and systems you have in place as 'what your PMO does', and rather consider them as 'services' you are offering your internal clients - would you select your offering over competing services on the open market?

Be honest here.

If yes, great.

If no, also great.

Either way – you are now thinking with the new frame of mind that you need to truly create a High Value PMO and embed it within your organisation.

...And, whether you mean to or not, you are now considering the Value Equation. Shown over the page, getting the Value Equation right underpins your success in creating sustainable and self-propagating processes and systems.

Thankfully, the Value Equation is nice and simple. It's 2 columns:

1) What your customers get (reward), and
2) How painful it is to get it (pain).

Clearly you want more pluses and less negatives, but there's some interesting science behind it.

The Interesting Science Behind It

Over the last half century behavioural studies of those suffering from chronic pain have found that we humans will actively avoid any activity that we fear will result in a painful experience.

No surprises there.

However, in 2012 a group of behavioural scientists at Ghent University in Belgium felt that the current pain-avoidance thinking was too narrow. They hypothesised that the findings to date on pain-avoidance were sorely[1] one sided; and that the decision to avoid or persist with a painful activity is likely affected by the level of motivational conflict at the point of decision.

In short – they wondered if we only avoid pain when we don't have a good enough reason to endure it.

So, they put together an experiment[2], and like all good experiments, it included zapping people with electricity. After gaining approval from the Ghent University's ethical committee – they were good to go.

The 56 undergraduate students that volunteered to participate in the experiment were promptly split into two groups.

---

[1] *Excuse the pun, I couldn't help myself*

[2] *Van Damme S, Van Ryckeghem DM, Wyffels F, Van Hulle L, & Crombez G (2012). No pain no gain? Pursuing a competing goal inhibits avoidance behavior. Pain, 153 (4)*

The first group of poor souls were the 'control' group. Their job was to demonstrate that undergraduate students were also pain adverse. They were strapped into a device that asked them to complete a series of simple number and letter based tasks. The catch was that on completion of 50% of these tasks, the participant received a mildly painful electro-shock. As you would expect, the group completed very few of these tasks.

The second group were deemed the 'competition' group. This group were provided a slightly different proposition - they were offered a monetary reward. After being strapped into the same device as the control group, this group were provided an incentive. Each time participants in this group were shocked, their input screen showed an increasing point score. The higher the point score, the higher the monetary reward they received.

The result: The second group willingly completed far more of the pain-inducing tasks.

If we translate this experiment into our Value Equation, the reason for this result becomes obvious. We end up with a Value Equation that looks something like this:

EXPERIMENT GROUP	WHAT YOUR CUSTOMERS GET (REWARD)	HOW PAINFUL IT IS TO GET IT (PAIN)
Control Group (no reward)	- The satisfaction of a completed task.	- A moderately painful electric shock
Competition Group (monetary reward)	- The satisfaction of a completed task. - A financial reward for each shock-fueled task completed. **PLUS** the researchers unintentionally added gamification elements which created: - A point-based dopamine hit. - The potential for point-based bragging rights among the participant's peers.	- A moderately painful electric shock

Simply put – there was a high task completion rate by the competition group because the value equation was balanced back towards the Reward Column. Completing the tasks and enduring the pain became 'worth it'.

Let's bring this back to PMOs.

Why PMOs Suffer from Adherence Issues

Almost every PMO I've worked with has suffered with adherence issues at one stage or another. The good news is I can tell you exactly what's going wrong.

As you might have already guessed, it's got to do with the Value Equation. Most PMOs build processes that look something like this:

PROCESS	WHAT YOUR CUSTOMERS GET (REWARD)	HOW PAINFUL IT IS TO GET IT (PAIN)
Project Reporting	- Avoid being hassled for reports. - Their project turns up on a dashboard.	- Potentially several hours of data collation and wordsmithing.

Net Result: Painful.

Or perhaps we should look at one of the most ignored aspects of project management I've ever come across – Lessons Learned. Most organisations just shove 'Lessons Learned' into their project closure reports – which then get filed away and forgotten about.

What are the chances we are getting good adherence or high-quality content in there? Let's look at the Value Equation for it.

PROCESS	WHAT YOUR CUSTOMERS GET (REWARD)	HOW PAINFUL IT IS TO GET IT (PAIN)
Lessons Learned Capture	- A slightly larger project closure document which may look a little more impressive. - Potentially, a tick in the 'project ready to close' check box by governing bodies.	- The effort to plan and run a workshop. - Provides an opportunity for difficult stakeholders to have a whinge. - Potentially hours of effort collating the workshop results into a report that is unlikely to be seen again. - High amounts of effort at the end of the project – when energy is low and executive focus has normally shifted away.

Net Result: VERY Painful.

Looking at the Value Equation – we start to see why most projects just tend to fade away rather than close and reflect. The value proposition is usually a deep negative.

So, What Can We Do?

We can use the information from our client clarity work to stack our Value Equations towards our clients. Your aim here is to create a balanced and more rewarding solution for them.

Let's have another look at the project reporting example we used earlier. Except, this time, let's assume this PMO has entered the High Value Service cycle (and is therefore continually improving their service offering), while ensuring ongoing focus on their Clients' success.

Their Project Reporting Value Offering may look something like the following.

For the Executives, the Value Equation is nice and strong.

PROCESS	WHAT YOUR CUSTOMERS GET (REWARD)	HOW PAINFUL IT IS TO GET IT (PAIN)
Project Reporting Service **(Executive)**	- On-demand project information. - Single source of truth. - Early indication of risks and issues. - Ability to focus on the strategic rather than the tactical.	- A minute to open a project dashboard and interact with it.

Net Result: Rewarding.

For the Project Managers, the Value Equation is similarly net Positive.

PROCESS	WHAT YOUR CUSTOMERS GET (REWARD)	HOW PAINFUL IT IS TO GET IT (PAIN)
Project Reporting Service **(Project Manager)**	- Project information readily available for sharing with executives and stakeholders. - A clear and simple way to escalate issues for discussion. - A pretty project dashboard showing all the elements that the project has under control – not just the parts that aren't.	- An hour a fortnight reviewing and adding commentary to a report that is partially pre-filled with easily accessible system data.

Net Result: Rewarding.

There are a few things you may notice here.

First, the process was renamed. It's now called the Project Reporting **Service**. The PMO in this example has shifted its focus from 'command & control' to service-centred. It now views reporting as one of the many ways it serves its client base. Like a vendor, it is therefore continually looking for ways to:

- increase the quality of its service,
- decrease the pain its clients feel in accessing the service, and,
- reduce PMO effort to offer the service.

For this PMO, this focus led to the purchase of an off-the-shelf project reporting toolset. The off-the-shelf solution automatically pulled information from disparate project sources so that the Project Manager and PMO didn't have to.

Second, the 'Reward' columns now outweigh the 'Pain' columns. This is because the PMO designed this service offering with the Value Equation in mind. It also focused on approaching the projects with a 'high trust' viewpoint. This changed the relationships with their project managers. It also reduced cumulative workload as it reduced the time it took to follow up reports.

Ultimately – this PMO shifted the tables from a net negative to a net positive. Any guesses on what this did for its adherence?

...If you guessed that it improved, then you would be correct.

DEVELOPING YOUR SERVICE OFFERING

Now you might be thinking:

'That all makes sense Brendon, but how do I use this?'

And if you are, then I commend you. That is absolutely the right question. After all, this is the section about clarifying your offering.

So, how do you achieve this clarity?

Well, as you may be starting to notice. I quite like simple. And developing your service offering is similarly simple.

To develop your service offering you must follow 2 steps.

1) Design a Service List, i.e., for each of the client archetypes you worked through earlier, you now need to come up with a list of services that:
    a. Will enable you to perform your purpose in solving their unique set of problems, and
    b. Are reasonably practical for your team and context.
2) Balance the Value Equation, i.e., for each of the services you designed in Step 1, consider your value equation. How can you make it as rewarding as possible for your clients while simultaneously reducing the pain endured to receive the reward?

Bonus Marks – Having Flashbacks?

For those of you who didn't skip the earlier parts of this book – what do the 2 steps above remind you of?

If you guessed the High Value Service Cycle, then give yourself an extra 10 points. Well done.

Shown below, the High Value Service Cycle shows how a truly effective PMO revolves through a version of these 2 steps on a regular basis to ensure ongoing innovation and continued usefulness.

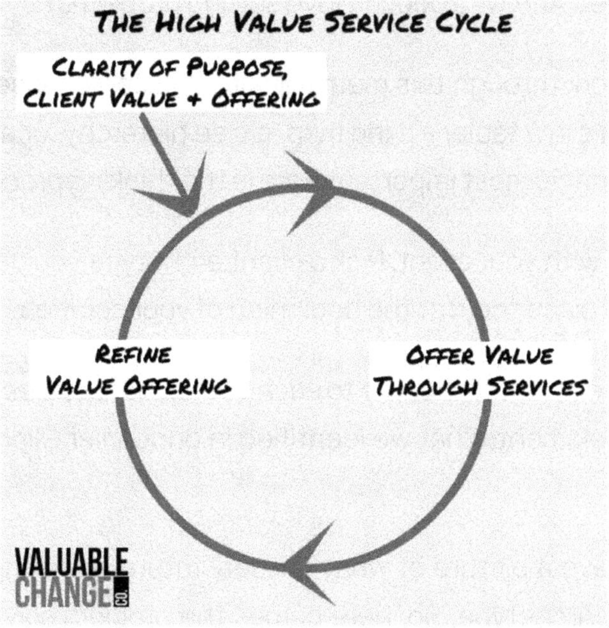

Step 1. Come Up With A Service List.

Yes, I know... on first blush, Step 1 seems a little on the nose.

> *'To develop a service offering, you must first come up with a service offering.'*

It almost feels a little like something Confucius may have said. Or perhaps Yoda...

What's interesting though is that Step 1 isn't what it first seems. Step 1 isn't just about making a list of services. Rather it's all about connecting solutions to problems and designing what the future will look like... And who doesn't love solving problems?!

So, let's work through this methodically. You can choose to work through this in a table, a mind map, a tree hierarchy, or any other toolset. What is most important here is the thinking process.

First, start with your client. Pick a client archetype you developed earlier and place them at the beginning of your solution.

Then connect that archetype to each of their '*What Does Success Look Like'* elements that we identified in our earlier Client Clarity work.

We now have a picture of what an ideal future is looking like for this Client Archetype. So, here comes the problem solving. How do we create that future for them by offering services?

How will your PMO create the environment needed?

How will your PMO enable the solution?

How will your PMO provide the guidance or even hands on support to achieve that future?

These are your services.

Then, for each service you plan to offer, answer the following questions. (Trust me, it's useful to do this upfront to help you prioritise PMO effort and resource planning in the future):

- What is your PMO's internal aptitude for that service? (i.e., is the service uniquely yours, or are you perhaps offering something that other units are also fully or partially offering?).
- What skills and systems are required to offer the service? (This will guide future investment planning).
- How will your client(s) access the service? (i.e., On request only? Self-service? Is it pushed to them on a schedule?)

To help you visualise this, over the page I have provided what the services for our Edwina Executive archetype could look like.

Adding to that, in the appendix at the end of this book, I've also provided a massive table of the various services that I've helped my client PMOs establish. Please feel free to draw on that for inspiration, however please note – you shouldn't feel that this list is exhaustive; so don't feel you are limited to just that set.

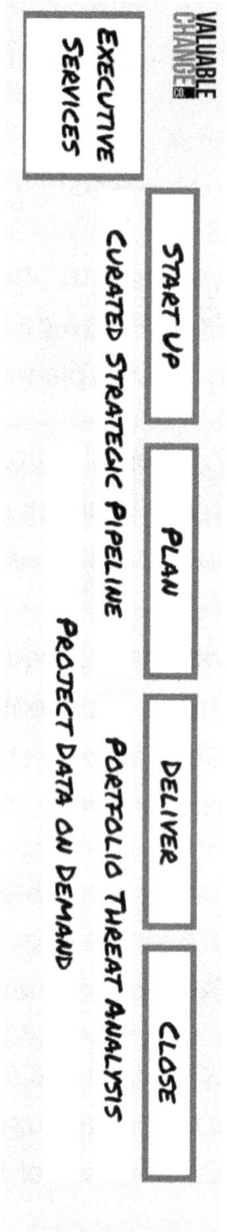

STEP 2. BALANCE THE VALUE EQUATION

Building from what we've just learned about reward vs pain, place each of your services into their own value equations. Then consider whether you are truly providing a service for your client (i.e., you are offering a net rewarding experience), or if you are providing a hindrance (i.e., a net painful experience).

This truly is the secret to a High Value PMO's ongoing longevity and success.

Now, here is where many of you may be thinking:

> *"But, Brendon surely we can't expect to offer a rewarding experience for EVERY service we're required to do, can we?"*

And my answer, as always is simple.

Only do this for the services you actually want people to use.

And only do this for the clients that you actually want to succeed.

The Third Step

Ok... Confession time.

I know I said there's only 2 steps to developing your service offering. And while that's technically true, you absolutely can create your service offering with just those 2 steps.

I would be remiss if I didn't tell you about what is probably the most important step: the 3rd one.

3) Map the services, make them easy to understand and then make the services well known and available to your clients.

A massive mistake most PMOs make is operating in isolation. Sitting in a group, surrounded by frameworks and templates. Discussing all the many ways they want to help their clients.

But they never actually tell their clients they can help.

Too many PMOs subscribe to the adage

> *"If you build it, they will come".*

When in all honestly, the adage should be:

> *"if you build it with them, then remind them about it, and publicise it widely, and then hold events, and generate buzz; then, maybe, they'll come."*

So how do we do this?

Well, strap yourself in ladies and gentlemen, because I'm about to suggest something a little wild.

Allocate time, money and people to communicating and promoting your service offering.

I know, wild huh?

And yes, for a medium to large PMO, I'm talking about one or more full time roles dedicated to promoting your service offering.

For smaller PMOs, this may just be an allocation of weekly effort. The trick for smaller PMOs is to cast your communications net smaller. Promote just as hard as the big PMOs, just to a smaller audience.

Now, so many of you will read this and think I've lost my mind. You're already understaffed, how can you justify time for promotion and communications. The answer is simple.

Revisit your purpose.

Select your client's top needs and blow away the rest.

Readjust your offerings to deliver ONLY those top needs.

Then promote these reduced services more clearly to your clients. And if anyone asks you do to something that is outside of your scope – the answer is easy: *'No... unless you plan to give more time and people to offer it with.'*

Feeling understaffed is just a result of a failure to say and stick to a firm 'No'.

Nice and Clear

Ok, you should now be nice and clear on your PMO's purpose, your client's needs and the services you plan to offer to create highly valuable results.

Now what?

Well, now we Rally the People.

CREATING HIGH VALUE PMOS
YOUR ESSENTIAL GUIDE

6

Step 2: Rally the People

Brian Cohen (of Nazareth) - *"Look, you've got it all wrong. You don't need to follow me. You don't need to follow anybody. You've got to think for yourselves. You're all individuals."*
Large Crowd - *"Yes. We're All Individuals!"*
Monty Python's the Life of Brian

Ready to hear something obvious?

You can't deliver success on your own.

Great, so now that we have established that, let's look at how you are going to ensure you have the support that you need to create a High Value PMO. This section is broken into 3 key parts.

First you must **Rally Your Team**. Your team is the backbone to your success. They will be with you through the highs and lows, so it is crucial to have them committed and onboard. To ensure you have that, I'll show you how to build momentum within your team, no matter the state of its morale.

Next you must **Rally Key Influencers**. These are the people that form the connective tissue of your organisation, which makes them the best people to recruit to your cause. To save you time, I'll show you the scientifically backed way to find these people using just 2 questions.

Finally, you must **Rally Your Community**. A functional community ensures ongoing growth and relevance for any PMO. So, I'll share with you the key components to building an attractive and sustainable community (i.e., one that doesn't fall apart after just 2 weeks!).

Rally Your Team: How to Build Internal Momentum

ELEVATING FROM DESPAIR TO CHANGE FANATIC

There's a concerning trend that I've seen across too many of my client's PMOs. The staff within these PMOs have grown worn, cynical and lifeless. It's usually the result of being stuck in the Administrative Death Cycle that we covered earlier in this book.

Often the staff can intuitively see the writing on the wall, but they are sticking around because, hey, at least it's a pay cheque.

However, even if your team isn't stuck in the depths of despair, not enough PMO staff are willing to stand at the top of a building and shout glory for their PMO! (...or at least talk up the cool things that their PMO is doing for their colleagues).

So, no matter where you and your team are, there is probably room for growth.

It's time to introduce to you to the Momentum Path (shown on the next page).

The Momentum Path enables you to diagnose the current momentum level of each member of your team[3], and then provides you a clear strategy on what to put in place to build to continue to grow.

---

[3] Yourself included.

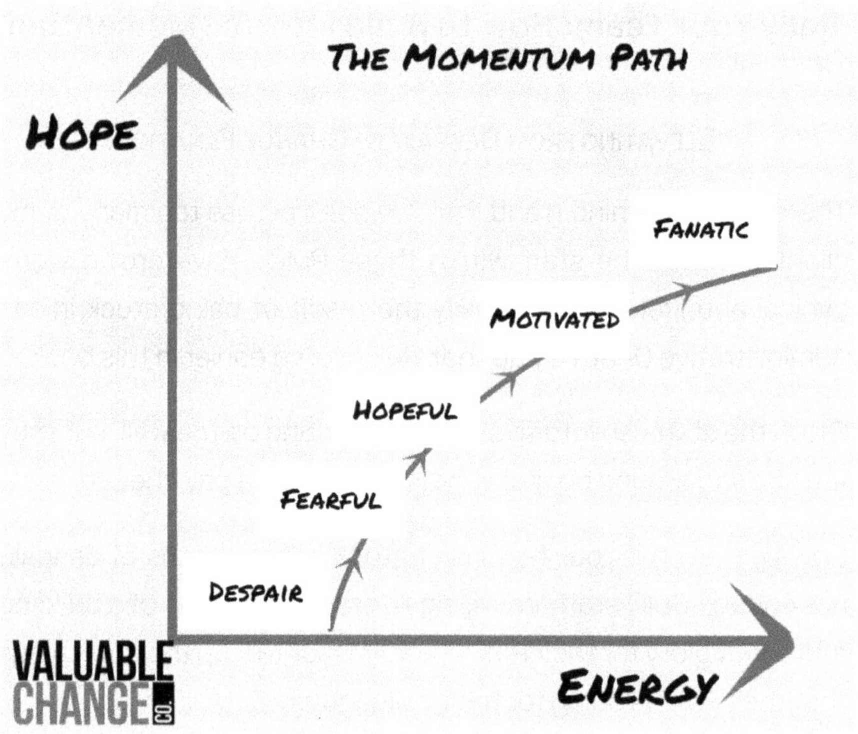

When considering momentum, you must look at two key elements – Hope and Energy.

For clarity here, I'm not talking about energy in a pseudo-science sense, or even an electrical one. I'm using the term energy closer the way that one could describe a 4-year-old child, i.e., 'Full of Energy'.

Hope, on the other hand can be thought of as a blend of the belief in the validity and usefulness of the work being done and an optimism for their personal future as part of this work.

What I've found is that the higher the energy and hope within your team, the higher the momentum. It makes sense then, that these two elements form the x and y axes for The Momentum Path. Plotted within you will find 5 levels:

- Despair,
- Fearful,
- Hopeful,
- Motivated, and
- Fanatic.

These 5 levels cover the breadth of momentum types that you are going to work with as you build a High Value PMO.

To put these into context for you, a team at its lowest point – Despair, has no interest in their work. They will be producing low to no useful output and will have no vacation or sick days left (as the days are taken as soon as they are available).

On the other hand, a team at its highest point - Fanatic will be eagerly engaging in each conversation, thriving with excitement to share new ideas. They will be talking about your PMO with friends and family. Teams with high momentum love coming to work, and truly believe in what they are doing.

Clearly, we want less Despair and more Fanaticism.

Identifying Where You (and Your Team) Are

Organisational energy is intangible – the measurement of which is not as simple as looking at a balance sheet (although sometimes there are some clues there).

Typically, qualitative measurements would need to be used here to gauge the levels of energy and hope. So, think surveys, focus groups, etc.

However, I've found that one of the most effective methods of gauging organisational energy is simply *observing*.

Momentum is felt rather than seen.

So, my advice here is trust your gut. If you've been working with your team for longer than a few weeks, then you will have picked up enough of a sense of the culture to be able to make a judgement.

But, for those who prefer a more analytical approach, feel free to release your inner Sherlock Holmes and look for clues in:

- The level of absenteeism,
- Time spent on non-work activity (e.g., surfing the internet),
- The general 'buzz' and franticness of your team – or a lack thereof,
- Regular high or low moods,
- An inability to deal with stress,

- High or low change resistance,
- Change fatigue and exhaustion.

Strategies To Level Up

What's interesting with the Momentum Path is that the strategy for one level is different to the strategy for another.

In other words, as Marshall Goldsmith says:

> *"What got you here, won't get you there".*

Let's spend some time together and explore what's needed to level up your momentum.

A quick note here before we dive into the specifics for each level. You may have noticed in the earlier diagram that the first few levels almost seem to stack on top of each other, then the last few spread out wide to the right. This is to reflect a crucial point.

Hope precedes Energy.

First, we must find ways to create Hope. Then, and only then, can we look to generate energy.

FROM DESPAIR TO FEARFUL

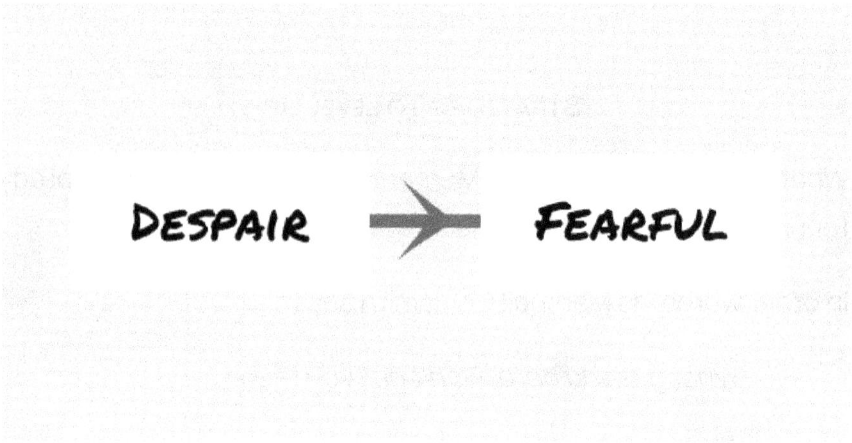

Those in Despair suffer from a complete and utter lack of hope. These people despise coming into work every day and are very likely miserable. They almost always feel stuck, because if they didn't, you can be sure they would have moved on already.

A primary factor for those in Despair is the feeling that their work at your organisation doesn't matter, so they have given up and will just do the bare minimum to get by.

Key Strategies for Those in Despair

We humans rarely change our minds without some form of new information or catalyst to excuse the change. This is especially so with strongly held negative views.

Your aim here is to discretely give those in Despair the **permission** to change their mind. None of us want to feel we are inconsistent, so there needs to be a notable change in something around them.

Give those in despair an excuse to build even the slightest semblance of hope again. This requires a physical change in either one or more of the following:

- Who (their team),
- What (their work),
- When (their timetabling),
- Where (their location), or
- How (their systems and processes).

Keep in mind though, that these changes will be met with absolute cynicism by those in Despair. The flicker of hope may not be obvious, but it will be there.

From Fearful to Hopeful

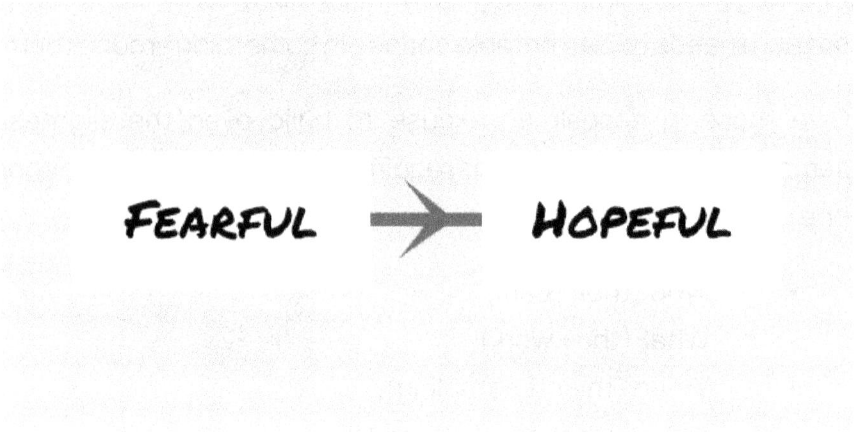

Those in Fearful have just a small seed of hope – they wish for more but are characterised by a disproportionate level of fear and skepticism.

Often fueled by previous experiences where they were left behind, embarrassed, or not considered – the work output from this group is also low, usually still only the bare minimum.

An extremely common theme for those in the fearful position is again a feeling that the work they do adds no real value to the organisation. However, unlike those in Despair, the Fearful haven't given up. Instead, they may well have good ideas but avoid instigating any change in case it places their position at risk.

Key Strategies for Those in Fearful

To create hope in this group we must attack on two fronts:

First, we must provide a way for them to complete low challenge but highly valuable work – with a clear linkage to organisational success. We are aiming to build up the belief that they do belong.

Second, we must address and overcome their fears. Key fears include embarrassment, trespassing norms, low skills, a lack of self-alignment, being taken advantage of, tall poppy syndrome and one of the worst - wasted and meaningless work. Use your intuition and empathy to dial in on which of the fears is at play. Then form a strategy to slowly counter the fear. The cultural techniques we will explore later in this book will also be invaluable here.

From Hopeful to Motivated

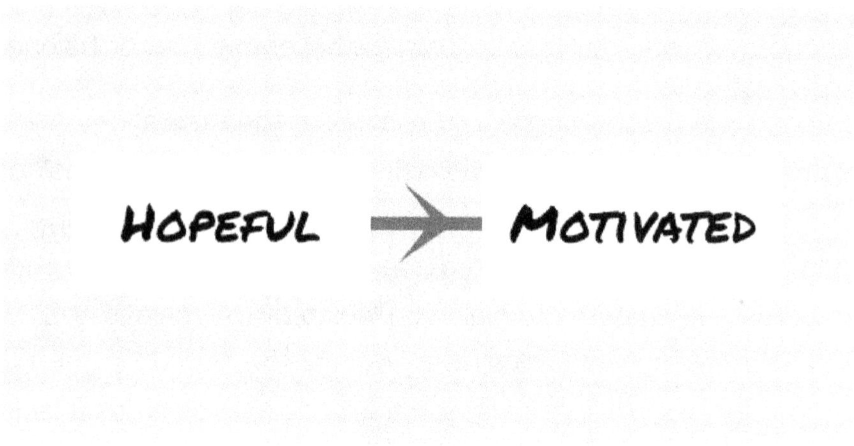

Those in Hopeful want to do good for the organisation but are risk-adverse. They are unsure of either their fit, contribution or skillset. Most new staff start here.

Key Strategies for Those in Hopeful

We are now transitioning from those that are skeptical of the organisation (Despair and Fearful) to those that are neutral and open. What this means for our strategies is that we are switching from a path of overcoming fears and baggage to one of generating motivation. Motivation is built on three key paths – challenge, empowerment, and clear contribution.[4]

Challenge: While we provided low challenge, high contribution opportunities for those in Fearful, those in Hopeful want to prove

---

[4] Which of course echoes the great work in Daniel Pink's *'Drive: The Surprising Truth About What Motivates Us'*.

'they can do it'. This means that they need an escalating set of challenges. Conquering one encourages progress to the next. Gamification strategies like 'levelling up' and tiered rewards can be useful to pursue and implement here.

Empowerment: We must provide those that are hopeful with the opportunity to self-select. What this means is that, while we may provide a path of increasing challenge, the Hopeful must be able to select and have input into what the next challenge will be. Two-way trust is essential here.

Clear Contribution: We must protect those that are hopeful against any backward slide that could be caused by meaningless work. It's crucial that their work has real meaning for the organisation and the PMO's forward movement. In other words, there must be a clearly visible path through the following.

Organisational Strategy - ›

Strategic Plan - ›

Personal Plan - ›

Personal Results - ›

Organisational Results

From Motivated to Fanatic

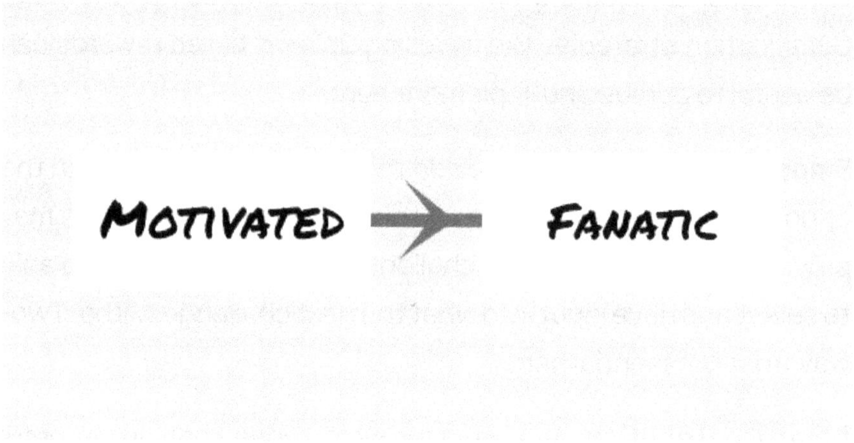

Those in Motivated are fantastic contributors for your PMO and organisation more broadly. They are highly reliable, self-driven members of staff who are taking action to ensure a good result for both themselves and your organisation.

There is, however, one step higher – 'Fanatic'.

Fanatics don't just like coming to work – **they love it.** Their obsessions drive them. They actively self-label as being a part of your organisation, not just working for it. They advocate internally for you with any staff that are at lower momentum levels, and are beacons of light within your area, groups and teams.

Key Strategies for Those in Motivated

Building Fanatics is difficult, second only to building hope for those stuck in Despair. The key strategies to build this group are:

- **Build a Shared Vision**: This includes involvement in not just decision but design. It includes co-design, radical knowledge sharing and regular feedback as you grow your PMO into a service-centred powerhouse.
- **Build Camaraderie**: Create mechanisms for sharing and recognition among their peers. This encourages ownership and will produce new ideas for your PMO.
- **Use targeted self-labelling and self-alignment**: Create a label that makes sense for this group to align with (e.g. 'Person X' is our internal expert on 'Topic Y'), and then provide them public exposure under that very label. No matter the result of the public exposure, these individuals will start to self-identify under that label. **Use this wisely.**

Maintaining High Momentum

Like an engine under power, your team's momentum can be 'revved higher' through the strategies we just discussed. However, similar to an engine – without proper care, the ongoing friction of everyday work will take its toll on your team's momentum.

Counter this by keeping in mind the two key measures for your team: Hope and Energy.

If you start to see or feel a drop in either of these, then it's likely that one or more of your team are sliding down the Momentum Path. Check in, evaluate where they are, and then reapply the strategies as needed.

The people in your PMO are responsible for every result your PMO produces. Don't waste them – build momentum, harness the talent, generate the energy – and watch your results improve out of sight.

Rally Key Influencers: How to Find the Right People in Your Organisation to Recruit to Your Cause

Introducing Internal Influencers

'Social Influencer' – a career that didn't exist just a few years ago is now a rapidly growing arm of the marketing efforts of businesses worldwide. With increases in dedicated influencer spend each year, projections suggest that between $5 and $10 Billion dollars were spent on influencers in 2020 alone.

It's clear that this group hold real power.

Social Influencers can take a multitude of forms – from beauty and fitness Instagram celebrities to video game streamers on Twitch or Vloggers on YouTube.[5]

But, not everyone wants to be an Instagram star. There are many who want to excel in finance, marketing, project management, leadership, or some other form of valuable service.

What's interesting for us is that, like social influencers in broader society, in every organisation there are key internal influencers scattered throughout. These people wield unbelievable power... and if you are serious about being a High Value PMO, then these are the people you need on your side.

[5] And even listing these channels here will slowly date this book as the brands grow, mature and then eventually fade away.

THE CONNECTIVE TISSUE OF YOUR ORGANISATION

Albert-László Barabási, a leading Professor of Network Science, found that no matter the network – from the grand expanse of the Internet to our own social groups – linkages form in the same patterns: Hubs and Nodes.

What results is something like the diagram below.

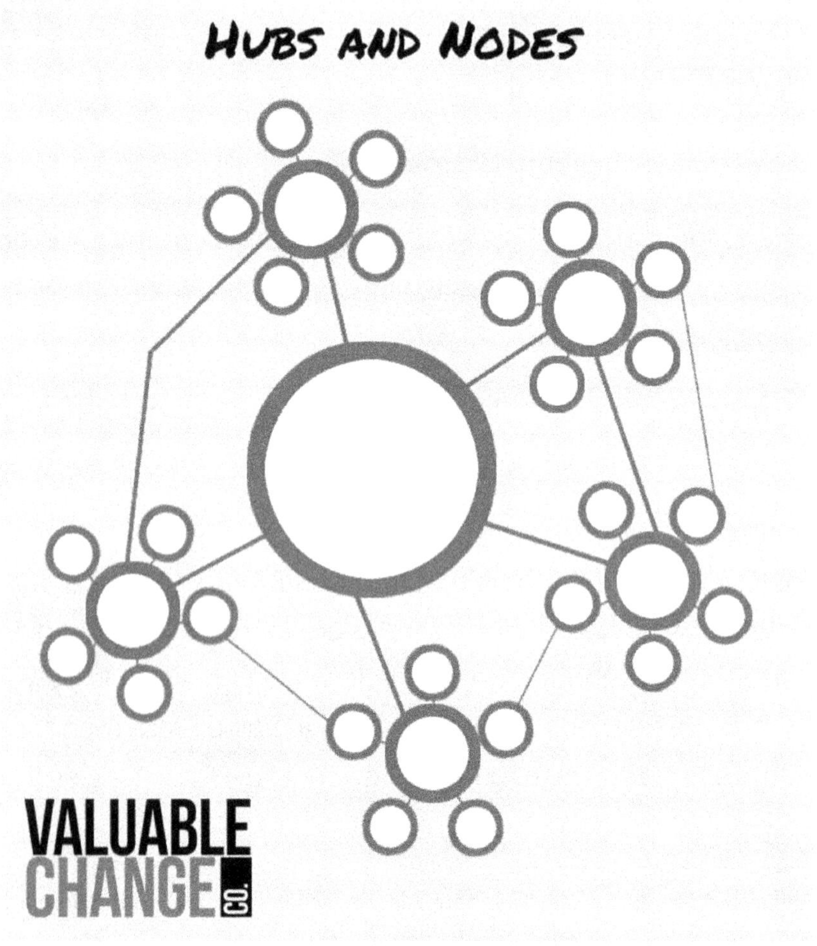

Here, let me prove it.

Take a moment and think about how you find most of your information and even access most websites online.

Do you manually type in the URL?

Sometimes perhaps – but most likely you find your information through one of the big connective Hubs. Google, Facebook, Bing or similar. On even cursory consideration, it's clear that the internet functions using this Hub and Node model.

Now, similar question – how do you find out information within your organisation? You probably go to just one or two people. These people are your information Hubs. Trace enough of these information connections and you would again start to see a picture of Hubs and Nodes.

What this means is that you have people in your organisation that are 'connection hubs' – people with a disproportionate number of social connections to the rest of the organisation. These people form the connective glue between staff.

Now reader, if you are strategically minded, you might already be starting to see the value of these connectors.

That's right – these are the people we want to help us implement our vision. By consciously recruiting and targeting these key connectors within our organisation we will both maximise our outreach (reducing the communication effort needed), while rear-guarding ourselves from the inevitable organisational politics that we all love to hate.

Now, you may be thinking here,

> *"That all sounds good Brendon, but how in the world am I going to find these people?!"*

Well, reader, are you ready to have your mind blown?

It's only going to take you 2 questions.

Finding Your Internal Influencers

It is at the intersection of two key types of people that we find our internal influencers:

- **Type 1: The Value Adders**. Value Adders are people that others love to work with because they carry more than their load, add something useful to every engagement and love to do so.
- **Type 2: The Information Brokers**. Information Brokers are the local go-to points for all relevant news, updates and (non-detrimental, honest) gossip.

The cool thing is, finding these people is surprisingly easy when you ask the right questions. The approach we are going to use is inspired by the concept of Snowball Sampling, a technique popular in statistics and sociology.

For any group that you are looking to identify the key internal influencers in, you merely need to run a simple survey that asks just 2 questions.

1) *If you could work with any three people from across the <group/branch/organisation>, on any project, who would they be?*
2) *If you needed to be filled in on organisational news, key updates or gossip, who would you go to first?*

Then all you need to do is collate the data. A simple tally of the names is enough to get started. The more times a name comes up, the higher that person's internal influence.

Simple right?

For the Data Nerds

For those data nerds amongst us (you know who you are), feel free to further query the information. Some other lenses to consider when examining the data include (but aren't limited to):

- Which organisational areas have the most influencers?
- Who are the highest influencers across multiple groups, within certain sets of interesting parameters?
- Which influencers have the most inter-team connections?
- Are the influencers slanted towards formal leadership roles or are they typically peer level?

ENLISTING YOUR INTERNAL INFLUENCERS

If you're in the PMO game, you're likely familiar with the concept of Change Champions. In case you aren't, here's a quick summary.

A Change Champion is typically someone outside of your team or project that is skilled up and enlisted as a peer-level support and flag-bearer within other teams or groups. They allow you to have a wider reach without needing to directly deploy staff into those areas.

This is exactly the approach to take for your newly identified Internal Influencers. Engage and skill up your influencers in your PMO offerings. Listen to their feedback and ensure you bring them 'under your banner'.

Rally Your Community: How to Ensure Your Community Doesn't Fizzle Out

THE ESSENCE OF A GREAT COMMUNITY

It might surprise you, but I can differentiate between communities that succeed and those that don't in just one sentence. And if you read the earlier chapter[6] on Clarity of Offering then you should be able to as well.

The key difference between communities that succeed and those that don't is the net balance of the value offering.

A typical PMO community falls flat because it doesn't stack the Value Equation in its favour. In other words, the events and benefits of the community don't outweigh the effort required to turn up, delay work, and persevere through awkward conversations.

So how do we stack the equation?

[6] And if you did skip it, then I highly recommend you go back and read it. This section will make far more sense if you do.

A Rewarding Community

There are 3 key avenues to boost the 'reward' column of your community's Value Equation:

1. **Exclusivity** – Your community can't be open to everyone. Counter-intuitively there needs to be barriers to entry. While these may not necessarily be financial (although they can be), a minimum criteria underpinning community acceptance is crucial. While this does increase the pain of access, it also ensures that the community consists of the right people. For a PMO Community that means targeting professionals who are actively interested in the community's success.

   With exclusivity we safeguard against dilution of value. We raise the lowest common denominator, which in turn, raises the value of the content you can and should explore. Exclusivity also sets your community up nicely to maximise the next two reward avenues.

2. **Reputation** – Your community must be held in high regard. It must be synonymous with success. The idea here is that anyone involved in your community receives a reputation boost simply by being connected to it. One of the best ways to achieve this is to identify high performers within your organisation and enlist them.

You should also put effort into leveraging popular and impressive names from the industry and have them speak to your members. You will increase your members' reputation just by correlating your community's name with a market leader. You want your members to be able to casually drop humblebrags[7] like:

"My mind is spinning. I still can't believe I got to meet the head of NASA's rocket program at the PMO Community Event yesterday!"

In short - you must provide ways for your community members to have a genuine advantage over those who aren't members.

3. **Edgy Content** - There is nothing worse than boring content. Want people to stop contributing to the community? Feed them yet another session on how to track capital expenses or the value of a change request.

   Content must be interesting. Instead of a session on the value of a change request – what about a session on '*How to avoid and shortcut our change request process*'?

   Can't come up with anything interesting? Ask an author to come talk. Or approach an industry legend. In other words

[7]Merriam-Webster: humblebrag: *to make a seemingly modest, self-critical, or casual statement or reference that is meant to draw attention to one's admirable or impressive qualities or achievements.*

– don't be afraid to outsource it. Worst case, I'm sure there's a consulting firm out there that would happily pull together the newest project management trends for you every quarter and present on it.

The point here is simple. **Don't be boring.** Don't just say the same old tired things. If you have pursued both of the Exclusivity and Reputation avenues, then you will have a membership of high performers.

Help them be even better.

Now, before we close this talk of community, here are a few other notes you should seriously consider.

- Your Community should have a brand. Something memorable and easy to verbally share. Your imagination really is the limit here, but as always, remember that simplicity is key.
- Maximise availability for members. Make the community hard to get into, but open and easy once you are in. Feel free to leverage the many social tools within your organisation here. MS Teams, Facebook for Workplace, etc.
- Opt for more impressive events, less often, rather than less impressive events, more often.

- There is massive value in connectivity. Not just to industry superstars, but also between organisational superstars. Create opportunities for their connection (without holding yet another networking event... **YAWN**).

- Ensure the small details are congruent with the image you're building. If your community is exclusive and has a high reputation - don't just put together the cheapest venues and food options. No one wants yet another Costco platter. However, a breakfast event at the local Hyatt – now that's another story.

- Give the community the time and investment it deserves. **DON'T** take on a community unless you have the ability to adequately support and promote it. This means at least a part time role allocation within your team and an appropriately sized budget to put behind it. You **will** have to spend money on this to succeed.

- Also, everyone thinks of a 'Project Management' community. But surely Project Manager's aren't your only client group. Consider how community (or communities) can best serve your **entire** client base.

Rallying is Hard Work

As you may be starting to see, rallying is hard work.

My advice here is don't shortchange yourself. Don't leave yourself with only expert schedulers and risk managers - leaving no one to create a solid PMO brand to rally behind.

As such, when you are designing the team that will support your journey to a High Value PMO, I highly recommend including a communications or marketing specialist.

Similarly, when seeking or allocating budget for this endeavour, ensure you put aside money for events and marketing.

You will thank me later.

7

Step 3: Avoid Cultural Traps

"Snakes. Why'd it have to be snakes?"
Indiana Jones, Raiders of the Lost Ark

Reader, it's time for us to revisit the tombs of the PMOs that came before us. Walk with me in this chapter and I will show you the traps that were laid. I'll shine a torch on the trigger wires that set off the arrow filled corridors, the touch plates that open the gaping spike pits, and the motion sensors that unleash the man[8]-eating scarabs.

In this step we will explore the top 4 killers of PMO effectiveness. Most of these are precursors to a slow but sure PMO death. So, for the High Value PMO, they are worth knowing about ahead of time.

Before we jump into the detail, let's take a brief look at these killers.

[8] Although, I suspect that the scarabs would devour all genders equally.

1. **An Ivory Tower Mentality** – This is by far the most common trap I've seen PMOs fall into. You find this trap at play when PMO staff spend long periods of time designing the 'perfect' framework and then demand that everyone follow it exactly. This is often epitomised in an 'us' and 'them' mentality.

2. **Dysfunctional Monopolies** – As we have touched on earlier in this guide, the PMO walks a thin line between useful and painful. This brings with it two key monopolistic traps to fall into. High Value PMOs must avoid becoming either a dictator or a slave.

3. **Stagnation** – Stagnation is a death by a thousand papercuts. Slowly time decays away the initial value offerings, and the organisation normalises what was previously a useful offering. High Value PMOs know how to keep moving forward – staying dry from the perpetual quicksand that is time.

4. **The 7 Deadly Fears** – Finally, a High Value PMO is one that is bold. There is no room for paralytic fear here. Yet fear is natural, so it will creep up in both ourselves and our teams. We must be ready to overcome each of the 7 Deadly Fears if and when they arise.

Trap 1: Building an Ivory Tower

The Ivory Tower is a metaphor with such a wonderful visual. A tower so tall, so protected, that it stands higher than the clouds. Truly isolated and disconnected from the world around it.

> *"To live or be in an ivory tower is not to know about or to want to avoid the ordinary and unpleasant things that happen in people's lives."*[9]

For a PMO, it represents a disconnect from their client base, with both the Project Managers at the metaphorical coalface, and the Executives steering the ship. After all, no project manager or executive cares all that much whether your latest risk management framework contains 4 or 5 steps.

Interestingly, Ivory Towers manifest within PMOs through two key means: Academic Self-Gratification and 'Us and Them' cultures.

Academic Self-Gratification

Academic Self-Gratification is the archetypal Ivory Tower. A group of usually bright people spending all day discussing complex ideas to complex problems, without actually achieving anything.

To paint you a picture here, let me tell you about one of the most dramatic instances of this I've ever seen.

---

[9] 'Ivory Tower' – Cambridge Dictionary.

A few years ago, a large government department set up a portfolio management office. Its mission was multifaceted and relatively undefined.

This PMO was special though. It had died and been rebirthed 4 times in just 6 years. That in itself is exceptional![10] For clarity here, when I say rebirth, I'm talking about a minimum 80% staff flush. This PMO had been through a lot over these iterations - from producing 40-page monthly status reports (and no, that's not an exaggeration), to producing absolutely nothing.

This PMO's latest iteration was particularly interesting for our discussion here. The PMO's leadership had a penchant for perfectionism. Couple this with a natural shyness and you end up with the greatest roadblock known to mankind. If we are talking Ivory Towers – then this PMO ended up building the Burj Khalifa[11].

This PMO had spent over a year with a team of 6 well paid contractors, writing, refining and then re-writing the PMO's library of frameworks and toolsets. Over this time not a single project had used, or even seen these frameworks or tools.

The PMO had managed to do something phenomenal - it had short-circuited the Administrative Death Cycle[12] by refusing to

---

[10] Unfortunately, exceptional for all the wrong reasons.

[11] The largest tower in the world at the time of writing – standing at 828 metres tall. Fun Fact – If you are ever in Dubai, I recommend going as high up as they'll let you. It's a fantastic view.

[12] Explained fully in Section 1 – The PMO Curse.

offer any sort of value at all! To give you a sense of the waste here - this PMO would be costing that organisation about $2 Million p/a in wages alone. And, while $2 Million isn't all that much in the project world – it's enough that you shouldn't be overtly wasting it.

Oh, and if you are wondering if I saw the frameworks that this year long concentrated effort produced – the answer is yes. All I can say is that if you had guessed that they were overworked and overly complex - then you would be correct.

While we will get to the strategies to counter Ivory Towers a little later, there is a quick moral to this story. As the Million Dollar Consultant Alan Weiss says:

> *"Progress not perfection. If you are at 80%, then move forward."*

Us vs Them

Us vs Them is a slightly different Ivory Tower. While Academic Self-Gratification is rather useless, Us vs Them towers are openly destructive.

For those of you lucky enough to have never seen an Us vs Them culture at play, let me tell you another story.

An ICT Project Management Office at a large, prominent Australian Federal Government Department were facing an uphill battle. Over the last few years many of their projects and project managers had shifted from Waterfall (sequential) to Agile (iterative) project delivery methods. However, the PMO had no agile experience, and were now stuck on how to support, monitor and govern the new delivery methods. Unfortunately, this disconnect wasn't viewed as a learning opportunity, but rather, it was creating a toxic 'PMO vs the World' culture.

Picture this. Your first day with this PMO. You are introduced to the team and given a walkthrough of their tools and systems. You are then informed, quite matter of factly that:

> *"The project managers are all idiots."*

How's that for customer service?[13]

---

[13] Of course, after 3 months of working with me, a phrase like that was seen as completely absurd.

An Us vs Them culture is dangerous because it creates an absolute misalignment between your PMO's goals and those of your clients. Further, it restricts your team's ability to empathise – accelerating your PMOs progress through the Administrative Death Cycle.

So, what can we do?

The counter to building an Ivory Tower can be summarised in just two words:

> Empathy and Experience.

The Ivory Counter: Empathy and Experience

The counter to an Ivory Tower is a 1, 2 combo. The good news is that if you're following the steps within this guide then you will have already completed the first step.

1. **Client Involved Co-Design**

   As we discussed in the sections earlier on 'Clarity of Client' and 'Clarity of Offering', it's crucial that you involve your PMO clients in the development of your PMO's offering. This isn't just to ensure that your offering solves an actual client need, but it also creates empathy within your team for your client's struggles.

   Until proven otherwise, you and your team should always assume that your clients are working with the best of intentions and to the best of their ability. Effective Co-Design sessions will give you a true insight into the struggles your clients are facing, and the role you and your team will play in resolving them.

2. **Staff Rotation or Shadowing**

   While empathy creating co-design is effective, there is nothing that speaks more to the creation of empathy than direct experience at the coalface within one or more projects.

A strong commonality across Ivory Tower PMOs is that all or most of the PMO staff usually have little to no real project experience. When you haven't been hands on with a project, then you can never really understand the imperfections of the reality the project managers need to operate within. Like the way that time is chewed up fighting figurative fires, and why the only way to keep the project registers up to date is by staying back and completing them at 10pm at night.

Without that understanding it is incredibly easy to get stuck in the theory.

So, to truly counter an Ivory Tower culture, a High Value PMO creates and then embeds a staff rotation program. Project Managers come into the PMO, and PMO staff rotate into the 'field'.

Not only does this rotation provide real time experience, but it also ensures a consistent stream of 'fresh blood' into the PMO. This fresh blood is often the catalyst for ongoing improvements to your PMO's services and solutions.

Now, if your organisation is one where a rotation program just isn't plausible, then consider establishing shadowing. Build into your staff and resource planning a 20% 'field experience allowance' where the staff in your PMO work with and for the projects you are serving.

Crumbling the Tower

An Ivory Tower culture is often an early indication that your PMO is on track for demise. However, a simple 1, 2 punch combo will effectively counter this.

The great thing is that these counters can be played both proactively and reactively. What this means is that no matter how tall your PMO Ivory Tower is – there is always a way back down.

Trap 2: Creating Dysfunctional Monopolies

Earlier in this guide we discussed your PMO's unique purpose, i.e., what is it that your PMO is best placed to offer?

The thing is, by focusing on our PMOs unique purpose, we are unintentionally positioning our PMOs to operate as an internal monopoly.

This is fine. Unlike in the open marketplace, we don't want massive duplication within our organisations.

However, as a monopoly, we must be responsible with how we choose to operate. By this, I mean, we must centre ourselves on the following spectrum.

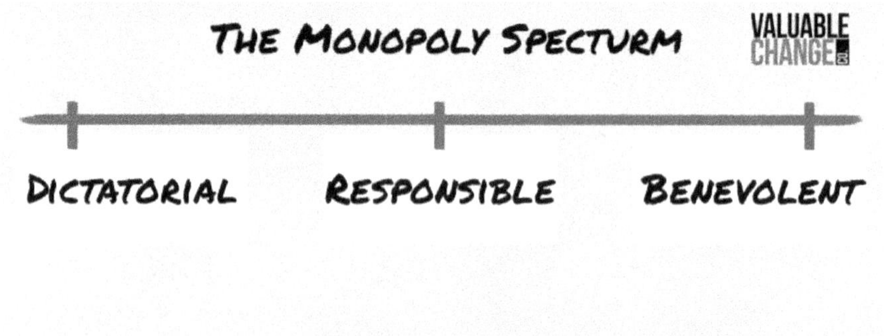

The Dictatorial Monopoly

We all know these units. The teams in these units seemingly start each day with a collective chant:

> *'It's our way or the highway'.*

Dictatorial Monopolies just don't care about, or have resigned themselves to, the negative value equation they offer.

Bolstered by their monopolistic status, I'm always amused by the sheer unfounded confidence these teams can have. When chatting to a future client that I suspected was running a dictatorial monopoly, I had one of their staff blatantly express to me:

> *"Our project managers are useless, as are our Executives. They never follow our processes."*[14]

Suspicions confirmed.

There are several indications that you might be running a Dictatorial Monopoly.

To explore these, let's do a quick 8 question quiz to see how dictatorial your PMO is. Each 'Yes' answer is 1 point.

---

[14] Hint – if your entire client base is 'useless', then it might be worth considering whether the problem is within your own team...

Q1: Is there a mismatch between your PMO's expectations of its client base, and what is reasonably required for project success?

Y/N

Q2: Is your PMO obsessed with the small, inconsequential details?

Y/N

Q3: Is your PMO adamant that detailed repetitive forms and long processes are absolutely crucial?

Y/N

Q4: Does your PMO have an Ivory Tower mentality (either Academic Self-Gratification or Us vs Them)?

Y/N

Q5: Does your PMO require things to be done '*because that's just how we do things*'?

Y/N

Q6: Do people dislike dealing with your PMO?

Y/N

Q7: Does your PMO have an automated email inbox response along the lines of "*we will get back to you sometime in the next 3 months*"[15].

Y/N

Q8: Does your PMO produce a net negative value equation across everything it administers.

Y/N.

So, how did you score?

A score higher than 2 is a strong indicator that your PMO has fallen into this trap.

However, a Dictatorial Monopoly is just one extreme of the monopoly spectrum. The other is a Benevolent (Slave) Monopoly.

[15] Yes, this example is all too real.

The Benevolent (Slave) Monopoly

These insidious units are harder to spot but are equally causing our organisations great harm. Like the Dictatorial Monopoly, the Benevolent Monopoly produces a negative value equation, however unlike the Dictatorially inclined, Benevolents don't make the direct client wear the pain. They absorb it into their own team(s) and push any overflow into the rest of the organisation via their other client groups.

Here's a very real example.

If I gave you an additional $560,000 a year, what would you do with it?

...Probably not this.

A portfolio manager was producing an organisation-wide project summary report on a quarterly basis. Unfortunately for this manager, the report was often bumped off her Executives' busy agenda. It was a tick and flick activity for the Executives who each viewed the report as low value, low pain.

What wasn't seen by these Executives was the pain in getting to that point. When you tallied the 40+ project managers' time and the multiple quality assurance steps this client's team undertook on the report – the organisation was wearing in excess of $140,000 each quarter to produce this routinely ignored report[16].

It was also a dreaded activity for all involved and distracted focus away from the delivery of the already in-flight projects.

Comically, this manager was considering doubling down on the pain and producing the report monthly!

The Benevolent Monopoly has an issue with, or rather an aversion to, saying 'No'. This has a knock-on problem – this type of monopoly says 'Yes' too much.

A PMO suffering from the Benevolent Monopoly trap endures the same problems that anyone who tries to make everyone else happy does:

- Overworked staff (often on inconsequential, and reactive things), which leads to
- An over-commitment that is passed onto their client base through delays, poor quality output and unreasonable turnaround expectations.

Ultimately, the Benevolent Monopoly sabotages the Value Equation of each of its offerings, not from a lack of care, but rather too much misplaced care.

---

[16] Among other strategies, placing a 'cost to produce' metric on the report notably reduced the executive bump rate.

Countering Dysfunctional Monopolies: The Responsible Monopoly

As we discussed earlier in the Guide, your PMO must think like a vendor, and like a vendor, your PMO must be continually looking for ways to:

- increase the quality of its service,
- decrease the pain its clients feel in accessing the service, and
- reduce PMO effort to offer the service.

These three steps are the crux of ensuring a responsible monopoly – in particular the last 2 points.

A Dictatorial Monopoly loses track of, or stops considering, the pain its clients feel in accessing the service.

A Benevolent (Slave) Monopoly fails to manage the PMO effort to offer the service.

Both monopolies ultimately reduce the quality of your PMO services.

So how do you stay responsible? Your PMO needs to review its position on each of these 3 points at least quarterly, if not more often.

Keep these goals front of mind and embed them into your PMO Values.

Trap 3: Stagnation

Interestingly, one of the largest threats to a High Value PMO is a fundamentally human trait: Normalisation and Adaptation.

In essence – even a High Value PMO can fall stagnant. Over time services become bland and expected, or worse, services become disconnected from client needs.

The context of your PMO changes each year, each month, and even each week. New executives, new projects and new organisational strategies all influence the effectiveness and alignment of your PMO's value offering.

Stagnation isn't a surprise to anyone... that is of course until it sneaks up on you.

Thankfully the High Value PMO has a key counter-strategy to stagnation: Learning.

The Counter Strategy: The Learning PMO

Learning.

We usually love to do it.

But, we usually don't love the work involved to get it.

The key question here is how do we embed learning into our teams, and then, maximise the payoff of doing so?

Now, if you have been around projects for a while then you will likely be well versed in the idea of a 'lesson learned'. For those of you that haven't been in projects for a while, here's a quick summary: When projects get to a key closure point (whether that be the end of an iteration, a stage or the entire project), the project team will sit back and reflect on what went well, and what didn't. The idea is that these reflections and learnings can then be passed forward to future projects to improve their chances of success.

The issue is – people aren't doing it.

Now your mileage may vary, but from what I've seen across the industry, at most, 35% of PMOs are asking their projects to capture lessons. Then only 2-3% of PMOs are actually sharing those lessons forward.

And 0% (i.e., none) of the PMOs are doing their own reflections.

Now if you are anything like me, then this may raise a few questions in your mind, like:

- What are the other 32% of PMOs doing with those project lessons they are asking the projects to capture? (Hint – they just file them away), and
- What's the point of going through those reflection processes if none of the lessons are ever seen again? (this is a very good question!).

But perhaps the most important question here is,

- How do we better learn from the past?

And this is the essence of what we are about to discuss.

Unfortunately, there is no secret sauce to embedding learning into our organisation. What we can do, however, is create the right frame, the right context and the right conversations. If you put these three elements into place you will maximise your chances of counteracting PMO stagnation.

THE RIGHT FRAME: PROOF OF LEARNING

There is a crucial idea that we must embed in our PMOs (and our projects too!). Simply put:

Writing a lesson down doesn't mean that we've learnt it.

What I'm saying here is that Identification =/= Proof.[17]

Just because we sat back and said:

> *"We could have done XYZ, which would have created a better result."*

is no guarantee that you or your successors won't repeat the same mistake in the future.

A better frame for our Learning effort is one that creates a separation between identification and learning. I often term these

---

[17] That is, Identification doesn't equal proof.

a Lesson Logged vs a Lesson Learned. But feel free to adjust the language as you see fit. What is important here is the frame.

Learning requires action, and ultimately, learning requires proof.

The Right Context: Fund Experimentation, Fund Growth

In order to have our staff learn, they need to be able to experiment. This requires funding and time.

I should be able to end discussion on this element here, because we all know we should be doing this already. We all know that we should be encouraging our teams to experiment and pursue new opportunities.

The problem is – most of us aren't doing it.

So, here is your gentle reminder that creating space for, and providing the funding to experiment is important when fending off stagnation. Allow your staff to try new things and then back them when they fail.

A truly High Value PMO sets the following as goals for its staff:

- Increase the quality of PMO services,
- Decrease the pain PMO clients feel in accessing the services, and
- Reduce PMO effort to offer the services.

...and then, it lets them run towards them.

And yes, this means budgeting for experimentation.

Reinforce this budget by taking a page out of 3M's famous playbook. Allocate a portion of time every week, month or quarter for experimentation and innovation.

For years organisations have battled with how to be more innovative. There's no secret here. Fund it, allocate time to it, then let your staff run.

Tip For Budgeting For Experimentation

There's no reason you need to call your budget allocation 'Experiments'.

'*Innovation*' is a fairly safe budget line, or for organisations too conservative for Innovation, try '*Operational Improvement*'.

The Right Conversations: Your Learning Journeys

I'm not going to claim credit for this idea, but unfortunately, I can't recall where I came across it. However, I would be remiss if I didn't share it with you as it's a technique that I've well and truly adopted into my toolbox.

But, before I share the technique with you, let me first ask you – how many times have you sat in a lessons review meeting, bored out of your mind, being asked the same old questions:

- What went well?
- What could we have done better?

Typically, these are framed against a series of categories. Time, Cost, Quality, Governance, and the like.

Have you ever sat there and wondered if there's a better way?

Well, there is. It is Learning Journeys.

The theory here is simple. We humans have communicated through story for as long as we have been human. Tap into this tradition by collaboratively telling the story of your PMO over the last week, month or quarter.

Rather than trying to remember what went well, create an interactive, evolving plotline. To do so, create a shared space for your team with a simple straight line.

Something like the below.

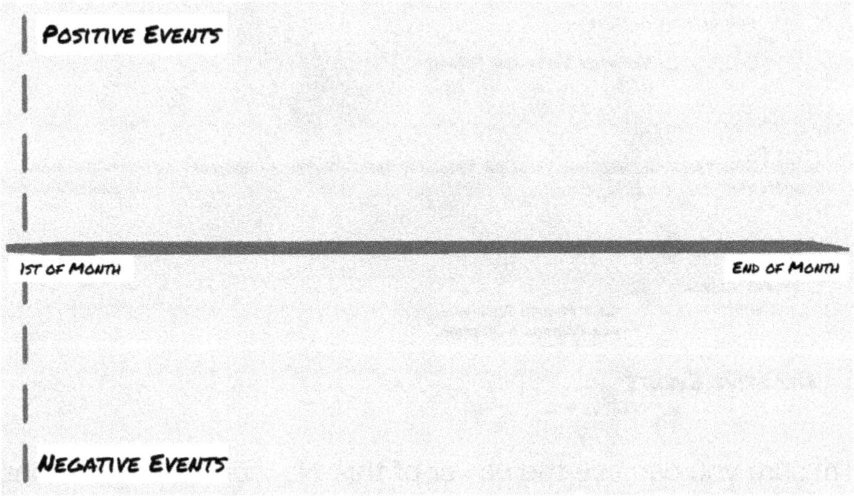

Then as the month[18] progresses, encourage your team to tell the PMO story on your interactive plotline. As an example, maybe you are 10 days into the month and your plotline is shaping up like the following.

---

[18] Or whatever time period makes sense for your PMO

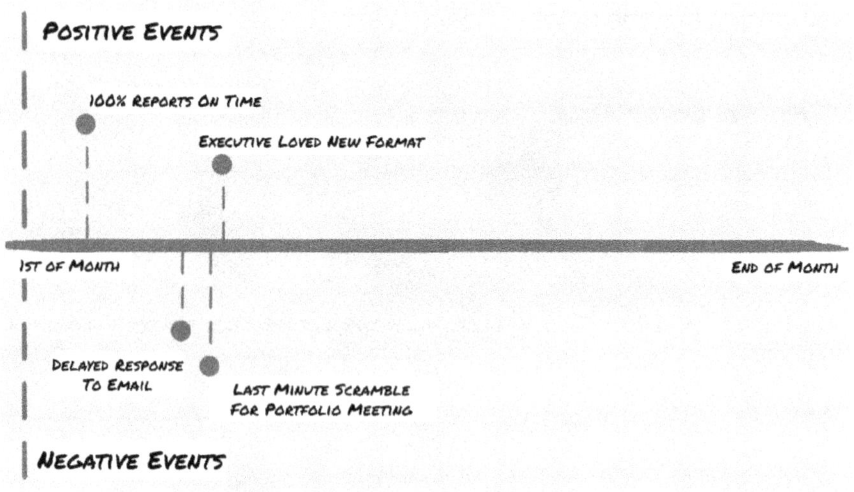

I'm sure you can see the power of this. No more pulling lessons from people like you would pull teeth.

This plotline tells the story of your PMO. Its highs, its lows. Ultimately, as you progress you will be identifying lessons as you are experiencing them.

Here's a few tips on Learning Journeys:

- When first introducing this practice, there is value in prompting and eliciting plot points in your daily standups or similar regular team meetings.
- Toward the end of the story period, you can hold a session to translate the plot into potential learnings. You can then build a plan to implement these learnings and compare your current journey against previous learnings to confirm they were in fact learned.

A Final Point on Stagnation

Avoiding stagnation is about ensuring your PMO continues to create and offer ongoing value for its client base. Learning is the key mechanic to counter stagnation. However, it's worth noting that a High Value PMO should also be regularly reviewing and updating its fit between client needs and its associated service offering (as a minimum, every 6 months).

Trap 4: The 7 Deadly Fears

I know, I know,

This is a book about PMO success, and yet, here we are talking about Fear.

But please stay with me here, because contrary to popular belief, Fear is truly destroying PMOs and it's terrible to see. The scariest thing is fear can debilitate your PMO in just 3 steps!

PMO kicks off & achieves early success.

-> One or more Deadly Fears infect the team(s).

-> The PMO clamours up and falls into one of the traps we've already explored.

Put simply, fear is often a precursor to the traps we've already discussed.

The Deadly 7

'The Deadly 7' - it sounds like a league of super-villains.

> *"Ah, you may have foiled us today Batman, but the Deadly 7 will get you next time!"*

Thankfully, this group of 7 don't wield super-powers. Their power instead comes from their insidious ability to stifle innovation, lower work engagement and diminish productivity.

The Deadly 7 are also scarily commonplace. As we work through each of the fears, take a moment to reflect on whether you have seen that fear play out in your career; either felt directly yourself, or vicariously through a colleague. I suspect that you will have seen most, if not all, of these fears at play. Let's briefly explore each one.

1. A Fear of Being Cut Down (Tall Poppy)

Our first fear is one that is particularly prevalent in my home country of Australia; Tall Poppy Syndrome.

Supposedly coined sometime in 1964, 'Tall Poppy Syndrome' is the levelling derision of anyone who thinks they should stand higher than everyone else. There are many claims to its origins, but I suspect that its roots in Australian culture formed as a rejection of the class structure inherited from our English heritage.

Tall Poppy is a great equaliser but suffers a major issue. More often than not, cultures that embrace a Tall Poppy mentality end up cutting down any person who seeks to be a standout success.

The net result of a team or individual suffering from this fear is an aversion to risk, not because they are afraid of the risk going wrong – but rather they are afraid of the risk going right!

No risk taking = stifled innovation, lower engagement, and diminished productivity.

2. A Fear of Meaningless Work

Anyone that has worked in a large, bureaucratic organisation likely knows the feeling all too well.

It's late on a Friday afternoon. You start packing your bag when a last-minute work request comes in. You sit back down, unpack, and start pulling it together. You even cash in some favours with your colleagues to get it done.

...Time passes, and you miss your social plans. But that's ok, because this work was urgently needed.

Finally, you complete your review, attach the document, and send the email. With a sigh of relief, you again pack your bags and enjoy your well earned weekend – only to come in on Monday and find out that:

> *"That last minute report? Oh, that was bumped from the agenda."*

No one even looked at it.

Yet another piece of work that will sit in a digital file, gathering digital dust. Never to be seen or used again.

It's a story that I've both lived and witnessed too many times.

This fear creates two major issues. The first, and most obvious – there is a notable amount of wasted work effort. Work effort that could be spent on other, more useful things. I do a lot of work with public sector organisations, and this is a huge problem in all of them. I haven't run the numbers, but I wouldn't be surprised if hundreds of thousands of staff hours are burned each year on examples just like the one above.

However, it's the second issue that is more insidious. Experiences like the one above create organisational cynics. The cynicism is a mechanism to hide the underlying fear – a fear of caring enough about something to put in the work, only for it to end up meaningless.

This protective cynicism isn't healthy. It's not selectively applied, and its often directed towards all work as it can be hard to tell ahead of time which bit of work will be ignored.

The net result again is an aversion to risk, stifled innovation, lower engagement, and diminished productivity.

3. A Fear of Insufficient Skill

Like the fears that came before it, a fear of insufficient skill is often masked by other protective personas, the most common being cynicism or a *'holier than thou'* approach. The individual experiencing this fear often deploys distractions to divert attention from their own ability, or lack thereof.

The essence of the fear is simple – it's a fear of not being skilled enough to succeed. If an individual doesn't feel they are *'good enough'* then that individual won't expose themselves to a risk they are sure they will fail.

Again, this fear creates a risk aversion, stifling innovation and lowering work engagement.

4. A Fear of Being Taken Advantage Of

Interestingly, the opposite to insufficient skill is also a catalyst for a fear – a fear of being taken advantage of. Anyone who is high in skill but low in assertiveness is particularly at risk here.

This fear is epitomised by the character 'Milton' from the 1999 cult-hit film Officespace. For those that haven't seen the film – Milton has an inability to firmly say no. Unfortunately, this means he ends up with without his stapler and desk that he doesn't want.

Thankfully, Milton is an extreme case, but like all good comedy, Officespace draws its inspirations from reality. When someone is scared they will be taken advantage of, they will often hide their talent, doing just enough to get by. Or, if their talent becomes known, they will work begrudgingly, lowering both productivity and innovation.

5. A Fear of Trespassing Norms

This fear is firmly rooted in your organisational culture. In short, your cultural status quo is a worthy adversary for any innovative mind. If the status quo is one that is risk adverse, or one that doesn't promote honest and open discussion, then your team(s) are unlikely to challenge ideas or overtly drive improvement for fear of being labelled the *'weird one'*.

6. A Fear of Embarrassment

A rather self-explanatory fear - a fear of embarrassment is a natural result of a lack of skill or cultural-fit.

No one likes being embarrassed, so they will avoid situations that place them at risk of being so.

7. A Fear of Personal Non-Alignment

This fear is a little different from the previous 6 and seems to be a much more modern phenomenon.

With the expansion of motivational speakers, personal coaches and an endless stream of aspirational content delivered to us through the internet – there is an increasing desire to *'do something fulfilling'*. While this is a valiant goal for us all to seek, unfortunately for many, doing something fulfilling is rooted firmly in fantasy, i.e., all passion, no challenge.

This shift in desire has introduced a new fear into our workplaces – a fear of personal non-alignment. Simply put, a fear of personal non-alignment is when someone holds themselves back from giving any more than, say, 60% of their effort into their work because they are concerned it is *'not one of their passions'*.

There are three key drivers underlying this fear:

1. A desire to avoid living a sub-standard life (against a glamourous but unrealistic social media benchmark).
2. A desire to live one's passions, but without any clear idea of what those passions actually are, and
3. A worry that one may well be genuinely talented at *'boring work'*... if one is good at boring work, then does that mean that they themselves are boring?

Interestingly, despite its recent origins, the end result of this fear is again a lack of engagement, risk aversion and stifled innovation. After all, who wants to put in extra effort into something that isn't *'speaking to them personally'*?

Countering the Deadly 7

Now, reader, you may have noticed something about each of the Deadly 7.

Each fear resulted in - stifled innovation,

- lower engagement, and
- diminished productivity.

This means that our approach to counter this 7 is to proactively counter these cultural shifts. We do this through normalisation of failure, success and meaning.

Let me share with you how I tend to do this.

Normalising Failure

First, reader, I have a question for you. When was the last time you truly failed? By this I mean gut wrenching, plate smashing, sleep destroying failure.

Has it been a while, or perhaps it's fresh and you are still sore from it? Either way, I bet you learned something valuable that you now share with others.

This is acute failure.

Acute failure is useful. We tend to create real behavioural shifts from it because we are often forced to. Acute failure is effective – but acute failure is expensive.

Interestingly, acute failure is what we often think about when we think of failure. So, when someone says to you that you should *'embrace failure'*, most of the time people tend to think of recovering better from acute failure.

But, what about the other type of failure? The subtle, everyday stuff. The comment that went over wrong at the meeting yesterday. The workshop that went 30 minutes overtime. The decision to buy fast food instead of bringing something pre-prepared from home.

Subtle failure is insidious, it adds up, but it doesn't cause notable change. It lingers. Subtle failures hardly ever see the light of day. No reflection, no storytelling, no growth.

This is the stuff that often slowly undermines your teams. As we build our High Value PMOs, it is this subtle failure that we need to try to normalise.

Here's how I often do it. I create a *'reflection point'* at the end of a day or week to provide the space and opportunity for your team(s) to expose the subtle failures. Its agenda typically looks something like this:

1) Tell us all a story of something that went terribly wrong today/this week, and some quick advice for your teammates from that experience. (30-45 seconds max per person).

However, it's the follow-up activity that's really powerful here. After the reflection point, write everyone's advice on a white board (or similar) that is visible to them for the following day/week.

Ensure the session is lighthearted, and that everyone gets a chance to share.

Through the simple act of exposure, storytelling and a little public accountability, failure becomes normal. When failure is normal, then there is far less to fear.

Normalising Success

Similar to normalising failure, we need to normalise success.

This is because a High Value PMO needs to be consistently pursuing success. This consistent pursuit often means going against the grain. When you are rowing upstream, your team(s) need to have the open and ongoing support of their colleagues.

So, to normalise success, I like to use a simple team gathering. It's a celebration of sorts – I call these *'Blow Your Own Horn'* sessions.

A Blow Your Own Horn (BYOH) session is a regular opportunity for your teams to meet and safely discuss the achievements they are most proud of that week.

The rules for a BYOH session are simple:

- Only one person speaks at a time.
- Everyone must share at least one thing they are proud of that week.
- They should speak boldly and be free to boast. Storytelling and hyperbole are acceptable.
- These are not feedback sessions, successes are celebrated, never refuted.

As you roll these out, there will be an initial awkwardness over the first few meetings as people adjust to the new self-promotional norm. This is where you, as a leader, must lead by example. Be candid and bold with what you share.

BYOH sessions attack the fears within your teams by providing them each social permission to grow.

Normalising Meaning

The final thing we must normalise is meaning, i.e., we must ensure our team(s) see the connection between their work and the broader vision and purpose.

Put another way, your team needs to deeply understand why they are doing what they are doing.

So, how do we normalise meaning?

Interestingly we do so through a blend of techniques that we have already explored in this Guide.

First, we create connection through our upfront and collaborative client co-design sessions.

Next, when building and assigning key tasks, we ensure that the 'So-What' is clearly defined and is openly discussed.

Finally, we should find ways to create organisational exposure for the meaningful work your High Value PMO is doing. This means identifying ways to mark and celebrate meaningful accomplishments.

You can also consider piggy-backing on your BYOH sessions by asking your team(s) to answer a so-what question on their personal weekly achievement. As a quick example: if the celebration is

> *'I found a way to eliminate half of the fields in one of our forms this week.'*

then the 'so what' is

> *'which means that our project managers will spend less time each month filling them out'.*

This type of 'so what' thinking regularly reconnects your team(s) with the greater client need they are helping solve.

A Quick Note on Meaningless Work

A High Value PMO is consistently pursuing a decrease in the PMO effort to serve. This means that your PMO should be actively eliminating meaningless work along the way.

A Final Note on Fear

Fear is normal and should be expected. The type of fear your High Value PMO will encounter will depend on your organisation's culture. However, as we have just discussed, fear doesn't have to be a death sentence for your PMO. Promote continued innovation, engagement and productivity by using the techniques we've discussed throughout this guide. In particular, ensure you normalise failure, success and meaning within your team(s).

YOUR PMO GAMEPLAN

8

A High Value PMO In Just 100 Days

"If you don't know where you are going, you'll end up someplace else."
Yogi Berra

What kind of project management book would this be without a good plan? I'm not one to leave you stranded with broad ideas – I'd much rather you actually implement these steps. So, this chapter contains how I personally tackle the establishment of, or evolution to, a High Value PMO. As always you are welcome to make it your own.

There are a few assumptions made in this plan, the key being that any new hiring has already been completed or will be run in parallel, and there will be no need for procurements or purchases of any kind during these 100 days.

Concentric Outreach – 3 by 30.

If I may, let me paint a picture for you on what you will need to do to create a High Value PMO. I want you to imagine three concentric circles, each larger than the last. These three circles represent the 3 key focus areas you will have to progress through to create a High Value PMO. The bigger the circle, the greater the integration with the rest of the organisation. The figure below gives you a sense of what I mean.

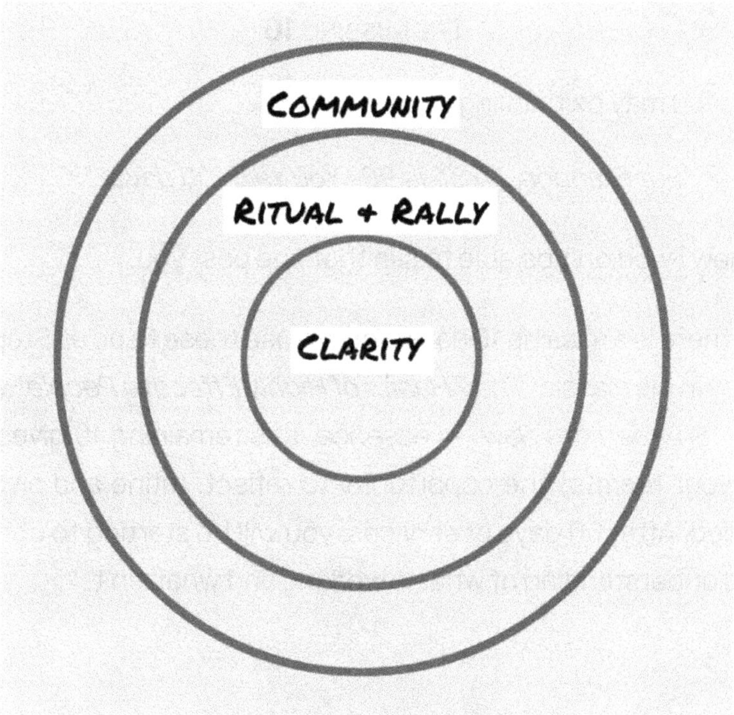

For the 100-day plan, each of these focus areas align with a group of 30 days.

This means that your first 30 days will be focused on Clarity, which is relatively insular, so it is shown as the smallest circle. The second 30 days expands your PMOs reach broader, focusing both inward (by embedding key rituals) and outward (by turning on services one at a time). This forms your second circle. Finally, the third 30 days is almost entirely focused outward. This 30 is where you build and leverage key connections throughout your organisation. This forms our third and largest circle.

THE MISSING 10

Now, you may be thinking:

> *"But Brendon, 3 x 30 is 90? You said 100 days?"*

...I knew I wouldn't be able to slip that one past you.

Yes, there is a missing 10 days. You will use these to do as Stephen Covey in his classic '*The 7 Habits of Highly Effective People*' would term '*Sharpen the Saw*'. In essence, this remaining 10 gives you and your team(s) the opportunity to reflect, refine and pivot as needed. After 60 days of services, you will be starting to obtain a good understanding of what is working and what isn't.

The First 30 - Clarity

It's likely no surprise to you that your first 30 days will focus on Step 1 of this guide – Clarity (Getting Clear).

In your first 30 days you will lay the foundations for your High Value PMO. This will mean the following:

- **Workshops:** Scheduling and running co-design workshops with your team and key stakeholders. These will be focused on progressing through the three key elements: Purpose, Client and Offering.
- **Service Map:** You will then leverage the results of these workshops into developing your service map. As you build your service map, ensure that you are tipping the balance of the value equation for each service to a net positive.
- **PMO Branding:** Finally, you will cap off your first 30 by establishing any PMO branding you plan to use. Branding can be useful for developing a high-performance reputation – just be careful not to become yet another acronym.

A.W.O.A. – A Warning On Acronyms

Anyone that has worked around large organisations for a while should be well versed in acronyms. Nothing represents this more for me than when, on my first day as a graduate, my required reading included a 10-page list of acronyms that were used by that organisation. To make it worse - this 10-page list was also out of date... by at least a year!

It's important to be careful with acronyms. A recent client had a branch named 'DIS'. For anyone that's even a little familiar with the US stock market, that's the stock ticker for Disney. This branch was henceforth nicknamed Disney, and a multitude of Princess and Star Wars jokes followed.

...I do doubt that's what they had in mind when they decided on 'DIS'.

The Second 30 - Ritual and Rally

Full warning, your second 30 days gets a bit busier...

The second 30 is where the rubber hits the road - you will be bridging the gap between standing up how your team will run while commencing PMO services.

This will mean:

- **Commence Services**: A High Value PMO offers value as soon as it possibly can. So, in the second 30 you will stand up your services. The trick here is not to do this in a big bang, but rather, think of it as a growing staircase. Each new service builds on the last. This approach allows you and your team(s) to be intentional and targeted with your rollout and communications. Trust me on this - this level of targeting will pay off in the long run.
  Note that it's ok to take your time here to get it right. Don't feel your PMO needs to deploy all of its services in its second 30. Remember its better to be good at a few things than mediocre at a lot.
- **Establish Team Rituals:** The second 30 is also crucial, as it's the first opportunity for your team(s) to operate in their new mindset. To reinforce this mindset, this is where you will set up and tweak the supporting rituals we have discussed through this guide.

In particular, you are establishing and embedding:

- Learning Journeys
- BYOH Sessions (Blow Your Own Horn)
- Failure Chats (Normalising Failure)

- **Rally & Promote:** The final thing that you will do in your second 30 is to commence your promotion and engagement efforts. These are ongoing activities, so your focus should be on setting them up and kicking them off. This will mean:
  - Creating communication channels (website, email inboxes, etc.)
  - Creating and commencing our communications and promotion plan(s).
  - Identifying the key internal influencers in your target client groups by running an influencer identification survey.

The Third 30 - Community

Your third 30 is where your focus shifts almost entirely to establishing and leveraging key networks throughout your organisation. Again, there are 3 key targets here:

- **Enlist Influencers**: Using the survey results from the second 30, approach the key client influencers to become champions for your PMO. Remember the value equation here - keep their role rewarding.
- **Create A High Performer Community:** Leveraging the principles discussed earlier in this book, set up a community for high performers that bridges one or more of your client groups. Remember: Exclusivity, Reputation and Content.
- **Establish Staff Rotation:** The final step of your third 30 is to establish your staff rotation program. Create ways to expose PMO staff to direct project experience, and project staff to the difficulties of PMO life. Rotations should be long enough to be meaningful, but not so long that they risk stagnation. 3 months is usually a good starting point here.

The Remaining 10 – Reflect & Refine

As mentioned earlier, the remaining 10 days are for reflection. Look back at your learning journeys, team failures and successes, then revisit your purpose, client map and service offering. Find areas that are disconnected or faltering, tweak them, and keep moving forward.

Your 100 Day Roadmap

For those of you that are visual, I've collated this gameplan into a lovely 'left to right' roadmap. Find this on the next page.

Your 100 Day Gameplan

First 30	Second 30	Third 30	Remaining 10
Clarity	Ritual + Rally	Community	Reflect + Refine
Run Co-Design Workshops	Establish Team Rituals	Establish Staff Rotation	Reflect, Refine + Pivot
Create A Service Map	Establish and Mature Services		
Design + Decide Branding	Create Comms Channels + Commnence Promotion	Create High Performer Community	
	Find Internal Inlfuencers In Client Groups	Enlist Influencers	

VALUABLE CHANGE CO

CREATING HIGH VALUE PMOS
YOUR ESSENTIAL GUIDE

9

A Final Note on PMOs

"I'm not dead yet!"
Monty Python and the Holy Grail

The last 20 years saw a surge in PMOs.

Then, the last 5 years saw their demise...

Or did it?

'Agile' methodologies were meant to kill off PMOs, and they succeeded for a while. But, cursed or not, PMOs are back.

Organisations still need help keeping up with the perpetual waves of change that they face every day. For as long as this is the case, there will always be a need to oversee, structure, support and guide our organisations through it. This is a role that a PMO, by any other name, can and should fill.

That said, the old style of PMO is dead. Command and Control styles of support have been doomed to obsolescence.

A truly High Value PMO is centred on service.

A truly High Value PMO balances their value equation towards rewarding their clients.

It's never too late to shift to Value. Whether your PMO is 3 days old or 3 years old, the techniques we have just covered will foster a PMO that truly lasts.

Just remember,

Have Courage.

No adventurer has ever overcome a curse by doing the same thing as everyone that came before them.

I wish you luck and success.

10

About The Author Brendon Baker

Brendon is converting others to a radical new idea... **Keep it simple.** We are all involved in changing our organisations, whether we know it or not. The issue is the industry has over-complicated it. From the obtuse jargon and untold reams of paperwork. It's just too hard, too confusing, and too academic. You don't have time for that. No one does.

As a leading expert in the field, Brendon Baker has consulted on over $10 Billion in key transformation projects and programs across a range of industries. This has included public infrastructure, business/cultural transformations, shared service implementations, restructures, process overhauls, technology deployments, social policy & more. Brendon Baker is the Managing Director of the Valuable Change Co. **His mission: Help Change Leaders Drive Real Value.** *www.valuablechange.com*

APPENDIX

The Massive List of Potential Services

Here is a massive, albeit non-exhaustive list of potential service offerings that a High Value PMO can offer.

In Alphabetical order.

- Additional / Continuation Funding Requests
- Agile Practices Advisory
- Agile Practices Training & Coaching
- Benefits Handover Support
- Benefits Management Training & Coaching
- Benefits Mapping Workshop Facilitation
- Benefits Monitoring Support
- Benefits Owner Support
- Benefits Owner Training & Coaching
- Benefits Profiling Support

- Benefits Training & Coaching
- Business Advisory Group Facilitation
- Business Case Review
- Business Impact Roadmap & Feedback Processes
- Change Governance Training & Coaching
- Close Assurance
- Close Notification
- Closure Checklist Review
- Closure Report Review
- Closure Support & Documentation Reviews
- Communities of Practice
- Cost Management Training & Coaching
- Curated Strategic Pipeline
- Exception Report Processes & Review
- Facilitate Governance Setup
- Gate Assurance Assessments
- Governance Setup Facilitation
- Health Checks - Deep Dive

- Health Checks - Light Touch
- Health Checks - Tailored
- Interdependency & Clash Advisory
- Interdependency & Clash Support
- Lesson Handover
- Lesson Search & Share
- Lessons Learned Workshop Facilitation
- Organisational Change Impact & Saturation Map
- Organisational Change Management Planning Consultation
- Organisational Change Readiness and Change Calendar Management
- Organisational PPM Skill Capacity Planning
- Planning Documentation Review
- PMO Anytime Contact & Triage
- PMO Concierge
- Portfolio Aggregation (Pipeline, Master Schedule, Risks, Issues, Quality Metrics, Resource Supply & Demand)

- Portfolio Fit Advice
- Portfolio Reporting (Pipeline, Master Schedule, Risks, Issues, Quality Metrics, Resource Supply & Demand)
- Portfolio Threat Analysis
- Post Project Implementation Review
- PPM Plan Review
- PPM Resource Pool / Farm
- PPM Systems & Toolsets Support & Training
- Procurement Support
- Project Cost Estimation Consultation
- Project Cost Monitoring & Advisory
- Project Data on Demand
- Project/Program Handover Facilitation
- Resource Demand Consultation
- Resource Management Advisory
- Resource Management Training and Coaching
- Risk & Issue Management Training & Coaching
- Risk & Issue Refresh Workshop Facilitation

- Risk Identification Workshop Facilitation
- Risk Plan Review
- Schedule Consultation & Review
- Schedule Management Advisory
- Schedule Management Training & Coaching
- Sponsor Training & Coaching
- Stage / Tranche / Phase Plan Review
- Stage / Tranche / Phase Report Review
- Stakeholder Buy-In Training & Coaching
- Stakeholder Impact Workshop Facilitation
- Start Up Documentation Review
- Status Report Review
- Strategic Change Alignment / Assessment
- Strategic Portfolio Management (Schedule, Prioritise)
- Writing A Good Business Case Training & Coaching

www.ingramcontent.com/pod-product-compliance
Lightning Source LLC
Chambersburg PA
CBHW071658210326
41597CB00017B/2237
* 9 7 8 0 6 4 5 1 2 2 7 4 9 *